AF879588

IN PROCEEDINGS BEFORE
THE UNITED STATES SENATE

In re:

IMPEACHMENT OF
FORMER PRESIDENT
DONALD J. TRUMP

TRIAL MEMORANDUM
OF DONALD J. TRUMP, 45TH PRESIDENT OF THE UNITED STATES OF AMERICA

Bruce L. Castor, Jr., Esquire
David Schoen, Esquire
Michael T. van der Veen, Esquire
Counsel to the 45th President of the United States

February 8, 2021

TABLE OF CONTENTS

I. INTRODUCTION

During the past four years, Democrat members of the United States House of Representatives have filed at least nine (9) resolutions to impeach Donald J. Trump, the 45th President of the United States,[1] each containing charges more outlandish than the next.[2] One might have been excused for thinking that the Democrats' fevered hatred for Citizen Trump and their "Trump Derangement Syndrome" would have broken by now, seeing as *he is no longer the President*, and yet for the second time in just over a year the United States Senate is preparing to sit as a Court of Impeachment, but this time over a private citizen who is a former President.[3] In this Country, the Constitution – not a political party and not politicians – reigns supreme. But through this latest Article of Impeachment now before the Senate, Democrat politicians seek to carve out a mechanism by which they can silence a political opponent and a minority party. The Senate must summarily reject this brazen political act

This rushed, single article of impeachment ignores the very Constitution from which its power comes and is itself defectively drafted.. In bringing this impeachment at all, the Members of the House leadership have debased the grave power of impeachment and disdained the solemn

---

1 Andrew Kaczynski, Christopher Massie, *A running list of Democrats who have discussed impeachment*, CNN (Mar. 12, 2017), https://www.cnn.com/2017/05/12/politics/kfile-democrats-impeach-trump/index.html

2 Some of the allegations that they thought were grounds for impeachment: national security decisions that were upheld by the Supreme Court, *see Trump v. Hawaii*, 138 S. Ct. 2392 (2018); publishing disparaging tweets about Democratic House members in response to their own attacks on the President, H.R. Res. 498, 116th Cong. (2019); and failing to nominate persons to fill vacancies and insulting the press, H.R. Res. 396, 116th Cong. (2019).

3 The charge itself is not even original: One of the articles of impeachment introduced by Representative Al Green back in December 2017 accused President Trump of "inciting hate and hostility" by "sowing discord among the people of the United States." *Impeaching Donald John Trump, President of the United States, of High Misdemeanors*, H.R. 646, 115th Cong. § 1 (2017).

responsibility that this awesome power entails. In bringing this impeachment in the manner in which they did, namely *via* a process that violated every precedent and every principle of fairness followed in impeachment inquiries for more than 150 years, they offered the public a master's class in the art of political opportunism.

The intellectual dishonesty and factual vacuity put forth by the House Managers in their trial memorandum only serve to further punctuate the point that this impeachment proceeding was never about seeking justice.[4] Instead, this was only ever a selfish attempt by Democratic leadership in the House to prey upon the feelings of horror and confusion that fell upon *all* Americans across the entire political spectrum upon seeing the destruction at the Capitol on January 6 by a few hundred people. Instead of acting to heal the nation, or at the very least focusing on prosecuting the lawbreakers who stormed the Capitol, the Speaker of the House and her allies have tried to callously harness the chaos of the moment for their own political gain.

II. STATEMENT OF FACTS RELEVANT TO THE ARTICLE OF IMPEACHMENT

On January 6, 2021, rioters entered the Capitol building and wrought unprecedented havoc, mayhem, and death. In a brazen attempt to further glorify violence, the House Managers took several pages of their Memorandum to restate over 50 sensationalized media reports detailing the horrific incidents and shocking violence of those hours. Counsel for the 45th President hereby stipulate that what happened at the Capitol by those criminals was horrible and horrific in every sense of those words. Their actions were utterly inexcusable and deserve robust and swift investigation and prosecution. As President Trump said in a video statement of condemnation, "I want to be very clear, I unequivocally condemn the violence that we saw last week. Violence and

---

4 Hugh Hewitt, *A fast-track impeachment would not be justice*, Washington Post (Jun. 8, 2021), https://www.washingtonpost.com/opinions/2021/01/08/fast-track-trump-impeachment-pointless-revenge/

vandalism have absolutely no place in our country and no place in our movement."[5] Mr. Trump's comments echoed his sentiments expressed the day of the rally, as he repeatedly urged protesters to stay peaceful,[6] and told rioters to go home.[7] [8]

The House Managers' compulsion to obfuscate the truth is borne out of an absence of evidence relied upon in their "Statement of Facts." As the body vested with the sole power to impeach, the House serves as the investigator and prosecutor. There was no investigation. The House abdicated that responsibility to the media. Of the 170 footnotes in the House Manager's Trial Memorandum, there were only three citations to affidavits of four law enforcement officers and they were merely referenced to support descriptions of what rioters were wearing and weapons that were found. The rest of the purported "facts" relied upon by these Constitutionally-charged prosecutors came from hearsay through the media.

---

5 Reuters, *Trump condemns Capitol Hill violence*, Reuters (Jan. 13, 2021).https://www.reuters.com/article/us-usa-trump-remarks/trump-condemns-capitol-hill-violence-in-video-that-does-not-mention-impeachment-idUSKBN29I37G

6 Rev.com, *Donald Trump Speech "Save America" Rally Transcript January 6*, Jan. 6, 2021, beginning at approximately 18:16 (emphasis added), available at https://www.rev.com/blog/transcripts/donald-trump-speech-save-america-rally-transcript-january-6. ("Transcript of January 6, 2021 Speech").

7 Kevin Breuninger, *Trump tells Capitol rioters to 'go home' but repeatedly pushes false claim that election was stolen,* CNBC (Jan. 6, 2021), https://www.cnbc.com/2021/01/06/trump-tells-capitol-rioters-to-go-home-now-but-still-calls-the-election-stolen.html

8 The House Managers' suggestion that President Trump did not act swiftly enough to quell the violence is absolutely not true. Upon hearing of the reports of violence, he tweeted, pleading with the crowd to be "peaceful," followed by a tweeted video urging people to "go home" and to do so in "peace." He and the White House further took immediate steps to coordinate with authorities to provide whatever was necessary to counteract the rioters. The fact is there are complex procedural elements involved in quelling a riot at the Capitol and on the mall – DC police, Capitol Police, National Guard, etc., There was a flurry of activity inside the White House working to mobilize assets. There is no legitimate proof, nor can there ever be, that President Trump was "delighted" by the events at the Capitol. He, like the rest of the Country, was horrified at the violence.

A. The Single Article Of Impeachment Is Belied By An Analysis Of Mr. Trump's Spoken Words To A Crowd Gathered At The Ellipse Four On January 6, 2021.

At the demand of the Speaker of the House, certain members of the House drafted and introduced Resolution 24 impeaching Mr. Trump, in his capacity as President of the United States. The single Article titled "Incitement of Insurrection" charged Mr. Trump with engaging in "high Crimes and Misdemeanors by inciting violence against the Government of the United States." Incitement is the act of encouraging someone to do or feel something unpleasant or violent.[9] An insurrection – unlike a riot – is an organized movement acting for the express purpose to overthrow and take possession of a government's powers.[10] President's Trump speech on January 6, 2021 was not an act encouraging an organized movement to overthrow the Unites States government.

On January 6, 2021, Mr. Trump addressed a crowd of people who had gathered on the Ellipse, public land that is part of the President's Park next to the White House. Mr. Trump spoke for approximately one hour and fifteen minutes. Of the over 10,000 words spoken, Mr. Trump used the word "fight" a little more than a handful of times and each time in the figurative sense that has long been accepted in public discourse when urging people to stand and use their voices to be heard on matters important to them; it was not and could not be construed to encourage acts of violence Notably absent from his speech was any reference to or encouragement of an insurrection, a riot, criminal action, or any acts of physical violence whatsoever. The only reference to force was in taking pride in his administration's creation of the Space Force. Mr. Trump never made any express or implied mention of weapons, the need for weapons, or anything

---

9 https://dictionary.cambridge.org/us/dictionary/english/incitement

10 Younis Bros. & Co. v. Cigna Worldwide Ins. Co., 899 F. Supp. 1385, 1392-1393 (E.D. Pa. 1995) (*citing Pan American World Airways, Inc. v. Aetna Casualty & Surety Co.*, 505 F.2d 989, 1017 (2d Cir. 1974) *Holiday Inns, Inc. v. Aetna Ins. Co.*, 571 F. Supp. 1460, 1487 (S.D.N.Y. 1983); and *Home Ins. Co. of New York v. Davila*, 212 F.2d 731, 736 (1st Cir.1954)).

of the sort. Instead, he simply called on those gathered to ***peacefully and patriotically use their voices***.

Mr. Trump greeting the crowd by remarking on the honor he felt looking out at the many "American patriots who are committed to the honesty of our elections and integrity of our glorious Republic." He went on to thank the crowd for their "extraordinary love" noting "that's what it is. There's never been a movement like this ever, ever for the extraordinary love for this amazing country and this amazing movement. Thank you." Mr. Trump told those gathered that "we're gathering in the heart of our Nation's Capital for one very, very basic and simple reason, to save our democracy."

Nearly twenty minutes into his speech, Mr. Trump said "I know that everyone here will soon be marching over to the Capitol building to ***peacefully and patriotically*** make your voices heard." Mr. Trump then spent approximately thirty to forty (30 – 40) minutes recapping some of his accomplishments as President and his beliefs on the outcome of the election, including the voting irregularities he attributed to the changes made in various states purportedly in response to the pandemic, and his conversation with Georgia's secretary of state.

As Mr. Trump was winding down his speech, he again looked out at all those gathered saying "looking out at all the amazing patriots here today, I have never been more confident in our nation's future." Although expressing some caution, Mr. Trump added "we are the greatest country on earth and we are headed, were headed, in the right direction." With great hope, Mr. Trump went on to state:

> As this enormous crowd shows, we have truth and justice on our side. We have a deep and enduring love for America in our hearts. We love our country. We have overwhelming pride in this great country, and we have it deep in our souls. Together we are determined to defend and preserve government of the people, by the people and for the people.

> Our brightest days are before us, our greatest achievements still wait. I think one of our great achievements will be election security because nobody until I came along, had any idea how corrupt our elections were. And again, most people would stand there at 9:00 in the evening and say, "I want to thank you very much," and they go off to some other life, but I said, "Something's wrong here. Something's really wrong. Can't have happened." And we fight. We fight like Hell and if you don't fight like Hell, you're not going to have a country anymore.
>
> Our exciting adventures and boldest endeavors have not yet begun. My fellow Americans for our movement, for our children and for our beloved country and I say this, despite all that's happened, the best is yet to come.

Mr. Trump concluded his speech at the Ellipse stating "[s]o let's walk down Pennsylvania Avenue. I want to thank you all. God bless you and God Bless America. Thank you all for being here, this is incredible. Thank you very much. Thank you." Despite the House Managers' charges against Mr. Trump, his statements cannot and could not reasonably be interpreted as a call to immediate violence or a call for a violent overthrown of the United States' government.

B. Democrat Members Of The House Drafted The Article Of Impeachment Before Any Investigation Into The Riot Had Even Started.

Democrat members of the House Judiciary Committee publically admitted that they began drafting the Article of Impeachment moments after angry extremists breached the doors of the Capitol.[11] The very next day, Speaker Nancy Pelosi and Senate Democratic Leader Chuck Schumer called on Vice-President Pence to invoke the 25th Amendment concluding – without any investigation – that Mr. Trump incited the insurrection and continued to pose an imminent danger

---

[11] Jennifer Haberkorn, *Sheltering in a Capitol Office: a California Lawmaker's Frantic Text Got the Impeachment Ball Rolling,* L.A. Times (Jan. 13, 2021), https://www.latimes.com/politics/story/2021-01-13/sheltering-in-a-capitol-office-a-california-lawmakers-frantic-text-got-the-impeachment-ball-rolling

if he remained in office as President.[12] Five days later, on January 11, 2020, House Democrats formally introduced House Resolution 24. On January 12th, Speaker Pelosi announced the nine representatives who would serve as the impeachment managers. One day later, on January 13th, House Democrats completed the fastest presidential impeachment inquiry in history and adopted the Article of Impeachment over strong opposition and with zero due process afforded to Mr. Trump, against Constitutional requirements and centuries of practice.[13]

C. The House Managers' "Statement Of Facts" Outlines A Narrative Irrelevant To The Facts Alleged In Support Of The Single Article Of Impeachment.

The House Managers spent nearly thirty-five (35) of their seventy-seven (77) page Trial Memorandum rehashing stories written by the media of mischaracterized statements attributed to Mr. Trump many months *before* Mr. Trump addressed the crowd at the Ellipse in Washington, D.C. on January 6, 2021. Media reports and reporters' opinions are not facts and most assuredly are not facts that should form the basis for instituting the grave power of impeachment. More significantly, however, Mr. Trump was never charged in the Article of Impeachment with the claims made in these various reports.

1. Law Enforcement Had Reports Of A Potential Attack On The Capitol Several Days Before President Trump's Speech.

Despite going to great lengths to include irrelevant information regarding Mr. Trump's comments dating back to August 2020 and various postings on social media, the House Managers are silent on one very chilling fact. The Federal Bureau of Investigation has confirmed that the

---

12 *Pelosi, Schumer Joint Statement on Call to Vice President Pence on Invoking 25th Amendment*, (Jan. 7, 2021), https://www.speaker.gov/newsroom/1721-0

13 H.Res.24 – Impeaching Donald John Trump, President of the United States, for high crimes and misdemeanors, 117th Congress (2021-2022), https://www.congress.gov/bill/117th-congress/house-resolution/24/actions

breach at the Capitol was planned *several days* in advance of the rally, and therefore had nothing to do with the President's speech on January 6th at the Ellipse. According to investigative reports all released after January 6, 2021, "the Capitol Police, the NYPD and the FBI all had prior warning there was going to be an attack on the Capitol..."[14] Embarrassingly enough, even members of the Democratic leadership themselves have admitted on the record, albeit subsequent to January 6, 2021, that they believed the riots were pre-planned, with some, including Representative James C. Clyburn, the House Democratic Whip, going so far as to accuse fellow House Members of coordinating and planning the attack in advance as co-conspirators.[15] The problem with that claim of course is that while the House Managers are clearly eager to make the most of this tragedy for their own purely personal political gain, House Leadership simply cannot have it both ways. Either the *President* incited the riots, like the Article claims, or the riots were pre-planned by a small group of criminals who deserve punishment to the fullest extent of the law. 33 Representatives are only now calling for investigations into Members across the aisle.[16]

---

14 Ian Schwartz, *John Solomon: Capitol Riot Was A "planned Attack," Can't Blame Trump; What Did Pelosi and McConnell Know?*, Real Clear Politics (Jan. 13, 2021), https://www.realclearpolitics.com/video/2021/01/13/john_solomon_capitol_riot_was_a_planned_attack_cant_blame_trump_what_did_pelosi_mcconnell_know.html

15 Geoff Earle, *Republican congressman's top aid admits to being with mob*, Daily Mail (Jan. 14, 2021),https://www.dailymail.co.uk/news/article-9147863/Democratic-whip-Jim-Clyburn-says-Democrats-convinced-MAGA-rioters-inside-help.html

16 Siladitya Ray, *Lawmakers Led "Reconnaissance' Tours of the Capitol,* Forbes (Jan. 13, 2021), https://www.forbes.com/sites/siladityaray/2021/01/13/lawmakers-led-reconnaissance-tours-of-the-capitol-ahead-of-last-weeks-riots-democratic-congresswoman-alleges/?sh=32ec8fe81c7e

The real truth is that the people who criminally breached the Capitol did so of their own accord[17] and for their own reasons, and they are being criminally prosecuted.[18] While never willing to allow a "good crisis" to go to waste, the Democratic leadership is incapable of understanding that not *everything* can always be blamed on their political adversaries, no matter how very badly they may wish to exploit any moment of uncertainty on the part of the American people.[19] Even a cursory investigation would have disproved the House's theory of incitement; however, Speaker Pelosi did not grant the President any of his Constitutionally mandated due process rights.

A simple timeline of events demonstrates conclusively that the riots were not inspired by the President's speech at the Ellipse. "The Capitol is 1.6 miles away from Ellipse Park which is near the White House. This is approximately a 30-33 minute walk. Trump began addressing the crowd at 11:58 AM and made his final remarks at 1:12 PM… Protesters, activists and rioters had

---

17 Some anti-Trump, some ani-government. *See, e.g.*, Alicia Powe, *Exclusive: "Boogaloo Boi" Leader Who Aligns with Black Lives Matter*, Gateway Pundit, (Jan. 17, 2021), https://www.thegatewaypundit.com/2021/01/boogaloo-boi-leader-aligns-black-lives-matter-boasted-organizing-armed-insurrection-us-capitol/. "The goal of swarming the home of the U.S. House of Representatives and Senate is **"to revel in the breach of security while mocking the defenses that protect tyrants…whether that be Trump or others."** *See also* Robert Mackey, *John Sullivan, Who Filmed Shooting of Ashli Babbitt*, The Intercept (Jan. 14, 2021), https://theintercept.com/2021/01/14/capitol-riot-john-sullivan-ashli-babbitt/ ("The rapper, who later retweeted a brief video clip of himself and Sullivan inside the Rotunda that was broadcast live on CNN, told me in an Instagram message … "I'm far from a Trump supporter…I really don't even get into politics at all. It was an experience for me and that's really the only reason I was there.")

18 *See, e.g.*, Tom Jackman, Marissa J. Lank, Jon Swaine, *Man who shot video of fatal Capitol shooting is arrested, remains focus of political storm,* Washington Post (Jan. 16, 2021), https://www.washingtonpost.com/nation/2021/01/16/sullivan-video-arrested/.

19 Over the last four years Donald J. Trump has been blamed for every manner of evil thing, and every crisis or news cycle that left people unsure of what to do was another opportunity to point a finger at the President. For one example, when a celebrity claimed that he was the victim of a violent hate crime, Donald Trump was blamed; and when it turned out that the claim was fraudulent the then-Mayor of Chicago quickly pivoted and *still* blamed President Trump for creating a 'toxic environment.' Howie Carr, *Trump is blamed for everything*, Boston Herald (Mar. 30, 2019), https://www.bostonherald.com/2019/03/30/fault-line-trump-is-blamed-for-everything/.

already breached Capitol Grounds a mile away 19 minutes prior to the end of President Trump's speech."[20]

2. The House Managers False Narrative Rests Entirely On Biased And Mischaracterized Reports By The Media And Cherry-Picked, Non-Contextual Parsing Of Mr. Trump's January 6 Speech.

Contrary to the false narrative set forth by the House Managers, Mr. Trump's speech was never directed to inciting or producing any imminent lawless action. It is important to read the speech in its entirety, because the House Managers played shamefully fast and loose with the truth as they cherry-picked its content along with content from other speeches made to other audiences for their Trial Memorandum, desperately searching for incitement and desperate to deflect attention away from the glaring inability to show an insurrection. And this is no small matter, because their demonstrably false claims go right to the heart of their main allegation.

Democrats cannot pretend that they were confused by the word 'fight' in the context President Trump used it in his speech; Speaker Pelosi has used this word multiple times herself in the context of election security,[21] and the well-known nonprofit started by rising Democratic darling Stacey Abrams and endorsed by none other than Speaker Pelosi[22] is literally called 'Fair Fight,' and it asks people to join the "fight for free and fair elections." And yet in her comments during the impeachment debate Speaker Pelosi adjusted the truth by conflating the parts of the

---

20 Tayler Hansen, *Independent Journalist Tayler Hansen: A Riot that Turned Deadly, What I Witnessed*, Gateway Pundit (Jan. 28, 2021), https://www.thegatewaypundit.com/2021/01/exclusive-independent-journalist-tayler-hansen-riot-turned-deadly-witnessed-us-capitol-riot/

21 Press Release, *Pelosi Remarks at Election Security Week of Action Press Conference*, Speaker.gov (Jul. 9, 2019), https://www.speaker.gov/newsroom/7819-2.

22 Press Release, *Pelosi, Schumer Announce Stacey Abrams To Deliver Democratic Response to President Trump's State of the Union*, Speaker.gov (Jan. 29, 2019), https://www.speaker.gov/newsroom/12919-3.

President's speech in which he talked about marching peacefully to the Capitol and the part of the speech addressing the need to fight for election security. She lied to the American people saying: "They were sent here, sent here by the president, with words such as a cry to fight like hell." Incredibly enough, her very next words were "Words matter. Truth matters. Accountability matters."

Words do matter and the words of President Trump's January 6th speech speak for themselves. President Trump did not direct anyone to commit lawless actions, and the claim that he could be responsible if a small group of criminals (who had come to the capital of their own accord armed and ready for a fight) completely misunderstood him, were so enamored with him and inspired by his words that they *left his speech early*, and then walked a mile and a half away to "imminently" do the opposite of what he had just asked for, is simply absurd. The attack on the Capitol was horrific. Period. But as constitutional professors[23] and experienced practitioners[24] agree, "The president didn't mention violence on Wednesday, much less provoke or incite it.[25] The fact that the House Managers found sheer deceptiveness necessary in the exercise of selectively parsing the words of the former President and quoting him out of context underscores the utter weakness of the House Managers' factual and legal claims. This tact is reminiscent of

---

23 Such as Andrew Koppelman, a Constitutional Law professor from Northwestern University, who explained "It seems to me the Brandenburg standard requires intention," and noted "It's like the word fight. It's often used as a metaphor. 'Senator X is a fighter. He will fight for you." Mark Sherman, Zeke Miller, *Can Trump be charged with inciting a riot? Legal bar is high*, Associated Press (Jan. 8, 2021), https://apnews.com/article/can-donald-trump-be-charged-incite-riot-3f27e4393e83d2967cf25bd18db5b268

24 Like Jefrey Scott Shapiro, a former District of Columbia assistant attorney general who has experience successfully – and unsuccessfully – convicting protesters for incitement. Jeffrey Scott Shapiro, *No, Trump Isn't Guilty of Incitement*, Wall Street Journal (Jan. 10, 2021), https://www.wsj.com/articles/no-trump-isnt-guilty-of-incitement-11610303966

25 *Id.*

Congressman Schiff's manufacturing of a fake conversation between President Trump and Ukrainian President Zelensky.[26]

Truth also matters very much. But Speaker Pelosi and her allies perverted the truth. The day after the riot, sensing a political opportunity, House Leadership decided to forego focusing on the business of the nation and unifying a bitterly divided country to once again endeavor to score political points against Mr. Trump. First, in an attempt to usurp Constitutional power that is not in any way hers, the Speaker demanded that Vice-President Michael Pence or the White House Cabinet invoke the 25th Amendment, threatening to launch an impeachment proceeding if they refused. Four days later, on January 11, 2021, an Article of Impeachment was introduced, which charged President Trump with "incitement of insurrection" against the United States government and "lawless action at the Capitol." See H. Res. 24 (117th Congress (2021-2022). The Speaker made good on her extortionate threat.

Accountability does matter, according to the House Managers, unless you are a Democrat. While fixating on words and sentences taken out of context, the House Managers ignore the many reckless statements made by their Democrat colleagues in the House and Senate. Merely by way of example, one need only search media reports to be reminded of Speaker Pelosi's 2018 hopeful comment when disagreeing with a policy: "I just don't even know why there aren't uprisings all over the country. Maybe there will be."[27] And just last summer, when sustained violent riots were

[26] Morgan Chalfant, Trump demands Schiff resign, The Hill (Sept. 17, 2019), https://thehill.com/homenews/administration/463344-trump-demands-schiff-resign.

[27] Douglas Ernst, *Nancy Pelosi wonders why there 'aren't uprisings' across nation: 'Maybe there will be,'* Washington Times (Jan. 14, 2018), https://www.washingtontimes.com/news/2018/jun/14/nancy-pelosi-wonders-why-there-arent-uprisings-acr/

decimating our cities and local businesses, Representative Ayana Pressley went on national TV and said that "there needs to be unrest in the streets."[28]

They also ignore the sheer hypocrisy of their House leader's 4-plus year quest to remove President Trump from office. After the Article was introduced, Speaker Pelosi again gave Vice-President Pence an ultimatum: either he invokes the 25th Amendment within twenty-four hours or the impeachment proceedings would proceed. Vice-President Pence responded in a letter to Speaker Pelosi the following day stating that he would not allow her to usurp constitutional authority that is not hers and extort him (and by extension the Nation) to invoke the 25th Amendment because he believed to do so would not "be in the best interest of our Nation or consistent with our Constitution."[29] Vice-President Pence also noted that Speaker Pelosi was being hypocritical, as she had previously stated that in utilizing the 25th Amendment, "we must be '[v]ery respectful of not making a judgment on the basis of a comment or behavior that we don't like, but [rather must base such a decision] on a medical decision."[30]

III. ARGUMENT

A. The Senate Lacks The Constitutional Jurisdiction To Conduct An Impeachment Trial Of A Former President.

The Constitution of the United States bifurcates the power of impeachment and addresses the issue in four places:

Article I, Section 2, Clause 5:

---

[28] Am Joy, *Post office cuts are wa against American people Pressley says*, MSNBC (Aug. 15, 2020), https://www.msnbc.com/am-joy/watch/post-office-cuts-are-war-against-american-people-pressley-says-90125893871

[29] See Mike Pence's Letter to Nancy Pelosi https://www.cnn.com/2021/01/12/politics/pence-letter/index.html.

[30] *Id.*

> The House of Representatives shall choose their Speaker and other Officers; and shall have the sole Power of Impeachment;[31]
>
> Article I, Section 3, Clauses 6 and 7:
> The Senate shall have the sole Power to try all Impeachments. When sitting for that Purpose, they shall be on Oath or Affirmation. When the President of the United States is tried, the Chief Justice shall preside: And no Person shall be convicted without the Concurrence of two-thirds of the Members present. Judgment in Cases of Impeachment shall not extend further than to removal from Office, and disqualification to hold and enjoy any Office of honor, Trust or Profit under the United States; but the Party convicted shall nevertheless be liable and subject to Indictment, Trial, Judgment and Punishment, according to Law;[32]
>
> Article II, Section 2:
> [The President] ... shall have power to grant reprieves and pardons for offenses against the United States, except in cases of impeachment;[33] and
>
> Article II, Section 4:
> The President, Vice President and all civil Officers of the United States, shall be removed from Office on Impeachment for, and Conviction of, Treason, Bribery, or other high Crimes and Misdemeanors.[34]

1. The Text And Structure Of The Articles Discussing Impeachment Do Not Grant To the Senate the Authority Over A Former President.

As is evident from our Constitution's plain text, Article II limits impeachment to current officials: "The President, Vice President and all civil Officers of the United States, shall be removed from Office on Impeachment for, and Conviction of, Treason, Bribery, or other high Crimes and Misdemeanors." As Alexis de Tocqueville wrote, impeachment was designed to

---

31 U.S. Const, art.1, § 2, cl. 5.

32 U.S. Const. art. 1, §3, cl. 6 and 7.

33 U.S. Const. art 2, § 2.

34 U.S. Const. art 2, § 4.

deprive a political actor "of the authority he has used to amiss."[35] In this instance, however, the Senate is being asked to do something patently ridiculous: try a private citizen in a process that is designed to remove him from an office *that he no longer holds*.

(a) The Impeachment of a Former President, A Private Citizen, Constitutes An Illegal Bill Of Attainder.

An impeachment trial of Mr. Trump held before the Senate would be nothing more nor less than the trial of a private citizen by a legislative body. An impeachment trial by the Senate of a private citizen violates Article I, Section 9 of the U.S. Constitution, which states that "[n]o bill of attainder . . . shall be passed."[36]

The Bill of Attainder, as this clause is known, prohibits Congress from enacting "a law that legislatively determines guilt and inflicts punishment upon an identifiable individual without provision of the protections of a judicial trial."[37] Simply put, "[a] bill of attainder is a legislative act which inflicts punishment without a judicial trial."[38] "The distinguishing characteristic of a bill of attainder is the substitution of legislative determination of guilt and legislative imposition of punishment for judicial finding and sentence."[39]

"[The Bill of Attainder Clause], and the separation of powers doctrine generally, reflect the Framers' concern that trial by a legislature lacks the safeguards necessary to prevent the abuse of

---

35 Katherine Shaw, *Impeachable Speech*, 70 Emory L.J. 1, 10 (2020), citing to ALEXIS DE TOCQUEVILLE, I DEMOCRACY IN AMERICA 101 (1838).

36 U.S. Const. art. I, § 9.

37 *Nixon v. Adm'r of Gen. Servs.*, 433 U.S. 425, 468 (1977).

38 *Cummings v. State of Missouri*, 71 U.S. 277, 323 (1866).

39 *United States v. Lovett*, 328 U.S. 303, 321-22 (1946) (Frankfurter, J., and Reed, J., concurring).

power."[40] As the Supreme Court explained in *United States v. Brown,*[41] "[t]he best available evidence, the writings of the architects of our constitutional system, indicate that the Bill of Attainder Clause was intended not as a narrow, technical (and therefore soon to be outmoded) prohibition, but rather as an implementation of the separation of powers, a general safeguard against legislative exercise of the judicial function, or more simply—trial by legislature."[42] The Bill of Attainder "reflected the Framers' belief that the Legislative Branch is not so well suited as politically independent judges and juries. . . " [43]

When the Senate undertakes an impeachment trial of a private citizen, it is acting as a judge and jury rather than a legislative body. And this is exactly the type of situation that the Bill of Attainder was meant to preclude. It is clear that disqualification from holding future office is a kind of punishment that is subject to the constitutional inhibition against the passage of bills of attainder, under which general designation bills of pains and penalties are included; in *Cummings, Ex parte Garland*, and *Brown*, the Supreme Court thrice struck down provisions that precluded support of the South or support of Communism from holding certain jobs as being in violation of this prohibition.[44] Thus the impeachment of a private citizen in order to disqualify them from holding office is an unconstitutional act constituting a Bill of Attainder.

---

40 *I.N.S. v. Chadha*, 462 U.S. 919, 962 (1983) (Powell, J., concurring opinion).

41 *United States v. Brown*, 381 U.S. 437, 442 (1965).

42 381 U.S. 437, 442 (1965).

43 *Id.* at 445.

44 *Cummings v. Missouri*, 71 U.S. 277 (1867)(noting that "[t]he deprivation of any rights, civil or political, previously enjoyed, may be punishment."); *Ex parte Garland*, 71 U.S. 333 (1866)(explaining that "exclusion from any of the professions or any of the ordinary avocations of life for past conduct can be regarded in no other light than as punishment for such conduct."); *see also Brown v. U.S.*, 381 U.S. 437, 458 (1965).

Moreover, this is the exact type of situation in which the fear would be great that some members of the Senate might be susceptible to acting in the haste the House did when it rushed through the Article of Impeachment in less than 48 hours, *i.e.*, acting hastily simply to appease the popular clamor of their political base.[45] As Chief Justice Marshall warned in *Fletcher v. Peck*,

> [I]t is not to be disguised that the framers of the constitution viewed, with some apprehension, the violent acts which might grow out of the feelings of the moment; and that the people of the United States, in adopting that instrument, have manifested a determination to shield themselves and their property from the effects of those sudden and strong passions to which men are exposed. The restrictions on the legislative power of the states are obviously founded in this sentiment; and the constitution of the United States contains what may be deemed a bill of rights for the people of each state. No state shall pass any bill of attainder. In this form the power of the legislature over the lives and fortunes of individuals is expressly restrained.[46]

2. The Constitution only gives the Senate Jurisdiction over the President, not the *former* President, of the United States.

One legal scholar described the simplicity of Article II's limitation, which House Managers try in vain to make seem inscrutable, in this way: "A half-grown boy reads in a newspaper that the President occupies the White House; if he would understand from that that all Ex-Presidents are in it together he would be considered a very unpromising lad."[47] That is the first reason why a former President cannot be impeached: he is not the President anymore.

As Professor Phillip Bobbit, one of the leading scholars on the impeachment process, and author of *Impeachment: A Handbook* (with Black, New Edition) (2018), recently argued:

---

45 *United States v. Brown*, 381 U.S. 437, 442 - 445 (1965).

46 *Fletcher v. Peck*, 10 U.S. 87, 137–38, 3 L. Ed. 162 (1810).

47 Brian C. Kalt, *The Constitutional Case for the Impeachability of Former Federal Officials: An Analysis of the Law, History, and Practice of Late Impeachment*, 6 Tex. Rev. L. & Pol. 13, 20 (2001).

> There is no authority granted to Congress to impeach and convict persons who are not "civil officers of the United States." It's as simple as that. But simplicity doesn't mean unimportance. Limiting Congress to its specified powers is a crucial element in the central idea of the U.S. Constitution: putting the state under law.[48]

Further textual support on this issue is evidenced by the Founders use of "shall" when identifying the penalty to be imposed, i.e. "...**shall** be removed from Office...." Justice Scalia once wrote, when the word "shall" can reasonably be understood as mandatory, it ought to be taken that way.[49] In 2007 the Supreme Court confirmed that

> The word `shall' generally indicates a command that admits of no discretion on the part of the person instructed to carry out the directive"); Black's Law Dictionary 1375 (6th ed. 1990) ("As used in statutes ... this word is generally imperative or mandatory").[50]

The text then is very clear: Conviction at an impeachment trial requires the possibility of a removal from office. Without that possibility, there cannot be a trial. In the civil law analogue, this case would be summarily dismissed under Federal Rules of Civil Procedure 12(b)(6), for "failure to state a claim upon which relief can be granted."[51]

The second reason a former President cannot be impeached follows logically from the first. The purpose of impeachment is to remove someone from office, and unequivocally, this impeachment trial is *not* about removing someone from office, as Mr. Trump left office on January 20, 2021. He is now, both factually and legally, a private citizen.

---

48 Bobbit, *Why the Senate Shouldn't Hold a Late Impeachment Trial,* Law Fare Blog (Jan. 27, 2021), https://www.lawfareblog.com/why-senate-shouldnt-hold-late-impeachment-trial#.

49 Scalia, Antonin; Garner, Bryan A. (2012). "11. Mandatory/Permissive Canon". *Reading Law: The Interpretation of Legal Texts* (Kindle ed.). St. Paul, MN: Thomson West. ISBN 978-0-314-27555-4.

50 *National Ass'n v. Defenders of Wildlife*, 551 U.S. 644, 661-62 (2007).

51 Fed. R. Civ. P. 12

House Managers have no authority to legally redefine "former Presidents" as "Presidents" for some constitutional provisions and not others. Would they accept a former President conducting foreign policy on behalf of the United States? Would they be content to have a "former President" nominate a Justice for a vacant seat on the Supreme Court? Of course not. That is why the term 'former President' is actually a term of art with legal ramifications, as evidenced by the Former Presidents Act (3 U.S.C. § 102 note), which states that:

> "(f)As used in this section, the term 'former President' means a person—
> "(1) who shall have held the office of President of the United States of America;
> "(2) whose service in such office shall have terminated other than by removal pursuant to section 4 of article II of the Constitution of the United States of America; and
> "(3) who does not then currently hold such office.

As it relates to the above definitional requirements, Mr. Trump has held the Office of President of the United States of America; his service was *not* terminated by removal pursuant to section 4 of article II of the Constitution (and even if this sham late impeachment were to result in a conviction, he *still* would not have been thus removed); and he does not currently hold such office. He is therefore *legally* in the separate category of 'former President' and is statutorily *not* the President of the United States referred to in the Impeachment Clauses of the Constitution. The text of the Constitution that provides only "[t]he President, Vice President and all Civil Officers of the United States, shall be removed from Office on Impeachment," supports the conclusion that the impeachment process applies only to officials in office.[52] This provision does not state "a" President or "a former" President, it unequivocally states "the" President. And when one refers to

[52] Harold J. Krent, *Can President Trump Be Impeached As Mr. Trump? Exploring the Temporal Dimension of Impeachments*, 95 Chi.-Kent L. Rev. 537, 540 (2020)(noting that RTILCE II "appears to limit impeachment of "officers" only when "removal" is possible, i.e., when the officer is still serving.")

"the" President, the reference is clearly to the current President. The text of the Constitution simply does not contain language allowing for the impeachment of a former President and does not address "late impeachments," i.e., an impeachment of a former officer.[53] Any inference from British practice about former officials is therefore a nullity because they *would* impeach private citizens, and our Framers decided *not* to do that. We chose not to remain British after all.

3. The Founders Knowingly Did Not Extend The Power Of Impeachment To Former Officials.

The Founders clearly decided to purposefully limit the power of impeachment in this way. The concept of a "late impeachment" was in use at the time the Constitution was written, with Great Britain specifically allowing impeachment of former officials.[54] In fact, the British Parliament could, and did, impeach private citizens. The Framers could have explicitly included a provision allowing for the impeachment of a former President, but they did not. Instead, the Constitution was written to restrict impeachment to specific public officials: "*the* President, Vice President, and other civil officers."[55]

"There is little discussion in the historical record surrounding the framing and ratification of the Constitution that treats the precise question of whether a person no longer a civil officer can

---

53 As stated in a recent report from the Congressional Research Service on "The Impeachment and Trial of a Former President": "The Constitution does not directly address whether Congress may impeach and try a former President for actions taken while in office," and "the text is open to debate." Congressional Research Service "The Impeachment and Trial of a Former President" https://crsreports.congress.gov/product/pdf/LSB/LSB10565 (Jan. 15, 2021).

54 Kalt at 25-26 (discussing state constitutions which specifically provided for late impeachments and quoting several constitutions which specifically provided for impeachment of an official "when he is out of office" or "either when in office, or after his resignation, or removal").

55 As argued by Jeremiah S. Black during Senator William Blount's impeachment: "A half-grown boy reads in a newspaper that *the* President occupies the White House; if he would understand from that that all Ex-Presidents are in it together he would be considered a very unpromising lad." 3 Hinds *Precedents of the House of Representatives*, § 2007 at 314 (1907). https://www.govinfo.gov/collection/precedents-of-the-house?path=/GPO/Precedents%20of%20the%20U.S.%20House%20of%20Representatives

be impeached—and in light of the clarity of the text, this is hardly surprising."[56] The text is also doubly clear given the clarity of available models in some of the United States themselves that *did* allow for late impeachments to take place.[57]

While the House Managers cite to some non-binding statements from John Quincy Adams about the possibility of late impeachment (in a case that did not even end with an impeachment) there is equal and perhaps even more on the scant record that would weigh against it. For example, as Professor Brian Kalt details, in multiple places Alexander "Hamilton seemed to believe that removal was a required component of the impeachment penalty, which suggests that he viewed

---

56 Bobbit, *supra.* https://www.lawfareblog.com/why-senate-shouldnt-hold-late-impeachment-trial

57 For example, the state Constitution of Vermont (7/1777) provides "the General Assembly [sic] of the Representatives of the Freemen of Vermont . . . may . . . impeach State criminals. Every officer of State, whether judicial or executive, shall be liable to be impeached by the General Assembly, either when in office, **or after his resignation, or removal** for mal-administration . . . Vt. Const. of 1777, ch. 2, § 20; or Pennsylvania (9/1776): "The general assembly of the representatives of the freemen of Pennsylvania . . . may . . . impeach state criminals. Every officer of state, whether judicial or executive, shall be liable to be impeached by the general assembly, either when in office, or after his resignation, or removal for mal-administration . . . .Pa. Const. of 1776, ch. II, §22.

As Brian Kalt explains, ideas like requiring a two-thirds majority to convict in the Senate are not self-evident, which is why the Framers took the time to spell them out. Late impeachment, so the argument goes, which is also not self-evident, would have also required specification if the Framers wished to include it as a possibility. Kalt at 37, see also *id* at fn. 441:

> See N.J. Const. of 1844, art. V, §11 ("The governor and all other officers under this State shall be liable to impeachment for misdemeanor in office, during their continuance in office, and for two years thereafter.") (emphasis added); Proceedings of the New Jersey State Constitutional Convention of 1844, at 600 (New Jersey Writers' Project ed., 1942) (chronicling last-minute addition of late impeachment provision); see also N.J. Const. art. VII, §3, cl. 1 ("The Governor and all other State officers, while in office and for two years thereafter, shall be liable to impeachment for misdemeanor committed during their respective continuance in office.").

Clearly late impeachment was something that people thought about, talked about, and wrote about, *if* they wanted to include it in their laws.

late impeachment as impossible."[58] In The Federalist No. 39, Madison wrote that the President of the United States is impeachable *at any time during his continuance in office*.[59] (Emphasis added).[60]

---

58 Kalt at 43.

59 Kalt at 50, citing The Federalist No. 39, at 397 (James Madison) (Clinton Rossiter ed., 1961). Kalt also notes that the other discussions of impeachment in The Federalist concerned removability, which buttresses the argument that impeachment was intended for sitting officers. *Id.* at 51.

60 Other states, like Georgia *had* late impeachment clauses up to a point and then and removed them. Kalt quotes the Georgia committee's discussion at length, noting that their consideration is very illuminating as an example of commonsense intuitions about the idea of a late impeachment:

> DR. PYLES: May I raise another question? What about this ". . . against all persons who shall have been . . . ." What's the point? . . This is highly confusing if you say ". . . shall have been in office . . . ." That's almost ex post facto or something.
> MR. CLARK: How can you impeach somebody who's not in office[?]
> DR. PYLES: Yeah. Or why. We've got criminal provisions, law, civil law.
> MR. CLARK: Any understandable background for that, that phraseology, "shall have been" ?
> CHAIRMAN SWEENEY: No.. . .
> MR. TIDWELL: If you look further into what you can do, the consequences are, he cannot hold office again. That might shed some light on that. . ..
> MR. HILL: . . . Now a person could leave office and two or three years later something is found out about that person that would be serious enough to warrant an impeachment trial so that he or she could never hold office again. . . . I don't think the language was happenstance, I think it was intended to cover both people in office and former officeholders.
> MR. CLARK: . . . [I]mpeachment is to put that person out of office, it seems to me, and the idea if he has committed some malfeasance or violation, that there would be criminal support, this falls into court action rather than the ponderous procedure of an impeachment. I just can't see it ever coming about . . . it clutters up again and adds questions to the Constitution that is just not necessary.
> MS. RYSTROM: I agree with you....
> DR. PYLES: I actually think the impeachment provision serves as a deterrent or maybe a threat against an officer, whether it will ever be carried out or not, the fact that it could be carried out is a pretty viable threat it would seem to me to an individual before he continued to persist in whatever it was that would be heinous enough to warrant impeachment.
> CHAIRMAN SWEENEY: Especially if he knows that it may come up after he leaves office.
> MR CLARK: . . . I don't think it's enough--it's not important enough to quibble about. I don't think it's likely to come up again, so I would be

Interestingly, where the Constitution refers to "the President" in Article 1, Section 3 and gives protocols for impeachment, such as "when the President of the United States is tried [in the Senate], the Chief Justice shall preside," the Senate reads this as applicable to the impeachment trial only of the current sitting President. Yet, under the House Managers' theory, they urge the Senate to read the constitutional provision that specifies "the President" is subject to impeachment to include a former President.[61]

4. Historical Precedents

(a) The Failed Attempts to Impeach Senator William Blount and Secretary of War William Belknap

The House Managers suggests there is "congressional precedent" for impeaching a former President in the impeachment cases of Senator William Blount and Secretary of War William Belknap. These two cases are actually inapposite and do not provide any binding precedential authority for impeaching a former President. .

In 1797, United States Senator William Blount of Tennessee faced allegations of conspiring to help Great Britain seize Spanish-controlled areas in Florida and what is now Louisiana as part of a scheme to pay off debts incurred from land speculation. Blount was expelled

---

> opposed to leaving the wording in there, I don't think it serves any protective purpose at all.
> CHAIRMAN SWEENEY: Well, is there a motion to drop it?. . .
> DR. PYLES: I so move.. . .
> CHAIRMAN SWEENEY: All in favor?
> MS. RYSTROM: I was getting convinced on the other side as this discussion went on.
> CHAIRMAN SWEENEY: Four [out of seven committee members present] in favor of dropping the language.

Kalt at 109-11, quoting from 2 State of Georgia Select Committee on Constitutional Revision, Transcript of Meetings, 1977-1981, Committee to Revise Article III, Oct. 29, 1979, at 29-30 (stating subcommittee's understanding that leaving office "obviate[s] the need for an impeachment proceeding."). Virginia removed late impeachment in 1830. See Kalt at 114, citing to Va. Const. of 1830, art. III, §13.

61 House Trial Memo. at 48-50.

by the Senate prior to his impeachment proceedings in 1798, he therefore argued that he was not subject to trial and refused to appear. Specifically, Blount argued that Senators or members of Congress could not be impeached, but only expelled by their respective chamber, and, even if Senators *could* be impeached, ex-Senators could not.

"In a close vote, the Senate defeated a resolution asserting Blount was an impeachable civil officer. But the debate around this vote, and the text of the resolution, do not make clear whether the resolution was rejected because it was felt that a senator was not "a civil officer" or whether, having been expelled, Blount ceased to be impeachable."[62] Therefore the case has little or no precedential value supporting a late impeachment.

In 1876, Belknap, Secretary of War under President Ulysses S. Grant, was investigated by the House for corruption. Belknap had accepted over $20,000 in kickbacks for the appointment of an associate to a lucrative military trading post at Fort Sill.[63] However, on March 2, 1876, after the House had taken up the issue but before the House voted on his impeachment, Grant accepted Belknap's resignation[64] – apparently just minutes before the House was set to vote.[65] Despite Belknap's resignation, the House voted to impeach him anyway. The issue of whether an officer who had resigned could be impeached was heavily debated from May15 to May 29th, but

---

62 *Id.*

63 United State Senate.gov https://www.senate.gov/artandhistory/history/minute/War_Secretarys_Impeachment_Trial.htm).

64 Of course the Belknap case is arguably different than Mr. Trump's because Mr. Trump did *not* try and escape a trial by resignation; this entire constitutional problem was created by the Democratic leadership that chose to wait until after his term had naturally expired.

65 *Id.*

ultimately the Senate voted 37-29 that it had the power to hold an impeachment trial for a former officeholder and proceeded to have a trial.[66]

On August 1, 1876, Belknap was acquitted because less than 2/3 of the Senate voted for impeachment.[67] While historical accounts suggest that few senators believed Belknap was innocent, the majority of those voting to acquit him did so **because they did not think the Senate had jurisdiction to convict someone who was no longer in office.**[68]

---

66 *Id.*

67 *Id.*

68 3 Hinds *Precedents of the House of Representatives*, § 2467 (1907):

> An analysis of the reasons given with the votes shows that of those voting "guilty," 2 believed that the Senate had no jurisdiction, but gave their verdict in good faith, since by vote jurisdiction had been assumed. Of those voting "not guilty,"3 announced that they did so on the evidence, while 22 announced that they voted not guilty because they believed the Senate had no jurisdiction. One Senator stated that he declined to vote because he believed they did not have jurisdiction.

As Alan Dershowitz framed this case and its relative import:

> No former official has ever been convicted by the Senate, and only one has been impeached. Secretary of War William W. Belknap was indisputably guilty of numerous impeachable offences, to which he confessed as he resigned his office hours before the House unanimously impeached him in 1876. The Senate voted in favor of a procedural motion affirming its jurisdiction to try Belknap's impeachment. But two dozen senators who believed he was guilty voted to acquit on jurisdictional grounds. A close vote nearly a century and a half ago doesn't establish a binding precedent.

Alan Dershowitz, *Senate Should Dismiss Article Impeachment Since Trump is Now Private Citizen,* The Hill (Jan. 21, 2021), https://thehill.com/homenews/media/535261-dershowitz-senate-should-dismiss-article-impeachment-since-trump-is-now.

There are also other recent precedents, in 1926 and 2009, in which judges resigned having been impeached, after which the House then petitioned the Senate to withdraw the indictment. See Bobbit, *supra.*, https://www.lawfareblog.com/why-senate-shouldnt-hold-late-impeachment-trial.

Significantly, neither Belknap nor Blount received the required two-thirds majority of the Senate and were acquitted so their proceedings provide no binding precedent establishing the Senate's jurisdiction to convict former officials of impeachment. "These cases cannot be read as foreclosing an argument that they never dealt with."[69] This is critically important because the burden of proof applies to both jurisdictional and substantive elements: "[T]he substantive elements of a federal statute describe the evil Congress seeks to prevent; the jurisdictional element connects the law to one of Congress's enumerated powers, thus establishing legislative authority. Both kinds of elements must be proved to a jury beyond a reasonable doubt; and because that is so, both may play a real role in a criminal case."[70] With impeachments, jurisdiction and guilt must be found by a two-thirds majority. Neither case established jurisdiction by the required two-thirds' majority. These two instances present, at best, an example of hypothetical jurisdiction.[71] It is also

---

69 *Waters v. Churchill*, 511 U.S. 661, 678, 114 S. Ct. 1878, 1889 (1994)(plurality). Furthermore, a court "is not bound by prior *sub silentio* holdings when a subsequent case finally brings the jurisdictional issue before us." *Will v. Michigan Dep't of State Police*, 491 U.S. 58, 63, n.4 (1989)(Court's alterations omitted) quoting *Hagans v. Lavine*, 415 U.S. 528, 535, n.5 (1977).

70 *Torres v. Lynch*, 136 S. Ct. 1619, 1630 (2016) (citations omitted).

71 *Steel Co. v. Citizens for a Better Env't*, 523 U.S. 83, 101-02, 118 S. Ct. 1003, 1016 (1998). The *Steel* Court discussed the threshold inquiry into jurisdiction noting contested questions of law could not be resolved when jurisdiction was in doubt:

> Hypothetical jurisdiction produces nothing more than a hypothetical judgment -- which comes to the same thing as an advisory opinion, disapproved by this Court from the beginning. *Muskrat v. United States*, 219 U.S. 346, 362, 55 L. Ed. 246, 31 S. Ct. 250 (1911); *Hayburn's Case*, 2 U.S. 409, 2 Dall. 409, 1 L. Ed. 436 (1792). Much more than legal niceties are at stake here. The statutory and (especially) constitutional elements of jurisdiction are an essential ingredient of separation and equilibration of powers, restraining the courts from acting at certain times, and even restraining them from acting permanently regarding certain subjects. *See United States v. Richardson*, 418 U.S. 166, 179, 41 L. Ed. 2d 678, 94 S. Ct. 2940 (1974); *Schlesinger v. Reservists Comm. to Stop the War*, 418 U.S. 208, 227, 41 L. Ed. 2d 706, 94 S. Ct. 2925 (1974). For a court to pronounce upon the meaning or the constitutionality of a state or federal

worth noting that neither of those cases dealt with a President, with his unique status in the Constitution, and with the clear definitional limits that apply to him and not to others.

(b) More Recent Impeachment Proceedings

In the past, Congress has acknowledged and exercised its duty to not impeach when an official is no longer in office. In the case involving the impeachment of President Richard M. Nixon, Congress decided not to impeach because he resigned from office. "[A]s a practical matter... the resignation of an official about to be impeached generally puts an end to impeachment proceedings because the primary objective—removal from office—has been accomplished." [72]

In May 1974, the House Judiciary Committee began formal impeachment hearings against President Nixon in regard to the Watergate scandal, and, on July 27, 1974, the House Judiciary Committee approved three articles of impeachment and reported them to the full House for consideration. Knowing that he was about to be impeached in the House and convicted in the Senate, Nixon resigned on August 8, 1974. The House officially ended the impeachment process against him on August 20, 1974, by accepting the committee's report, but deciding not to further advance impeachment proceedings.

As professor Bobbitt explained: "Why didn't they go ahead and impeach him when he resigned? The answer is they didn't believe that they had the authority to impeach someone who could not be removed, someone who was no longer, as the [constitutional] text requires, a 'civil officer' of the United States."[73] A memo from the Office of Legal Counsel at the time reached a

---

law when it has no jurisdiction to do so is, by very definition, for a court to act ultra vires.

72 *House Practice: A Guide to the Rules, Precedents and Procedures of the House*, Chap. 27 Impeachment § 2 at 604-05.

73 Interview with Columbia Law professor Philip Bobbitt, co-author of Impeachment: A Handbook (https://www.npr.org/2021/01/18/957866252/can-the-senate-try-an-ex-president).

very similar conclusion "[a]s a practical matter, if the President should resign, this would probably result in termination of impeachment proceedings."[74]

(c) State Courts Have Rejected Claims Similar To Those Made By The House Managers In Similar Late Impeachment Matters.

While the Supreme Court has not yet addressed the question of a late impeachment, some state courts have. In *State v. Hill*, the Supreme Court of Nebraska dealt with the exact same substantive question facing the Senate now, on almost identical Constitutional language. They addressed head on and dismissed the same claims that the House Managers now make. First, they started with the plain meaning of the word *officer* at issue:

> It is urged by counsel for the managers that ex–officers are liable to impeachment for official misdemeanors committed while in office; that jurisdiction attaches immediately upon the commission of an impeachable offense; and that the expiration of the official term does not deprive the legislature of the power to impeach, or the court to try. It cannot be said that there is any provision of the constitution which expressly confers the authority to impeach a person after he is out of office; while section 5, already quoted, designates the persons who may be impeached as "all civil officers of this state." This language is unambiguous. It means existing officers,—persons in office at the time they are impeached. Ex–officials are not civil officers within the meaning of the constitution. Jurisdiction to impeach attaches at the time the offense is committed, and continues during the time the offender remains in office, but no longer.[75]

Then the Court proceeded to address the question of disqualification as a separate remedial punishment:

> The necessary implication of the provisions in section 14, art. 3, of the constitution, that "judgment in cases of impeachment shall not extend further than removal from office and disqualification to hold

---

[74] U.S. Department of Justice, *Legal Aspects of Impeachment: An Overview, Volumes 1-5*, https://books.google.com/books?id=tHyQAAAAMAAJ&printsec=frontcover&source=gbs_ge_summary_r&cad=0#v=onepage&q&f=false.

[75] *State v. Hill*, 55 N.W. 794, 796 (Neb. 1893).

and enjoy any office of honor, profit, or trust in this state," is that the offending party must be in office at the time the impeachment proceedings are commenced. In case of impeachment, either one of two judgments can be pronounced, namely, removal from office, or removal and disqualification to hold office. It is obvious that there can be no judgment of removal where the party was not an officer when impeached. It is claimed by counsel for the managers, as we understand their argument, that a judgment of disqualification can be entered without a judgment of removal. All will concede that disqualification to hold office is a punishment much greater than removal; so that, if the construction contended for by counsel is the true one, then, in case the person impeached is out of office, he is liable to a more severe penalty than might have been inflicted upon him had he been impeached before he went out of office. We cannot believe that the members of the convention who framed the constitution so intended. Judge Story, in discussing the question whether a person can be impeached after he has ceased to hold office, at section 803 says: "As it is declared in one clause of the constitution that judgment in cases of impeachment shall not extend further than a removal from office, and disqualification to hold any office of honor, trust, or profit under the United States, and in another clause, that the 'president, vice president, and all civil officers of the United States shall be removed from office on impeachment for, and conviction of, treason, bribery, or other high crimes or misdemeanors,' it would seem to follow that the senate, on the conviction, were bound in all cases to enter a judgment of removal from office, though it has a discretion as to inflicting the punishment of disqualification. If, then, there must be a judgment of removal from office, it would seem to follow that the constitution contemplated that the party was still in office at the time of impeachment. If he was not, his offense was still liable to be tried and punished in the ordinary tribunals of justice. And it might be argued, with some force, that it would be a vain exercise of authority to try a delinquent for an impeachable offense, when the most important object for which the remedy was given was no longer necessary or attainable; and, although a judgment of disqualification might still be pronounced, the language of the constitution may create some doubt whether it can be pronounced without being coupled with a removal from office." [76]

[76] *Id.* at 796-97. Next the Court "rejected the British cases of Hastings and Melville as irrelevant given the broader scope of English impeachment… [and] rejected the Belknap precedent because of the weakness of the Senate's majority and also because, unlike Belknap, Benton and Hill were out of office from the natural expiration of their terms." Kalt, at 117; see also *id.* at fn. 454: describing how "in a case decided the same day, the court dismissed another late impeachment on different grounds, while noting its argument in Hill. *State v. Leese*, 55 N.W. 798, 799 (Neb. 1893) (citing Hill and pointing out that the legislature had no power to impeach Leese because he had been out of office for two years)."

The most recent state court opinion on late impeachment is *Smith v. Brantley*,[77] a Florida case from 1981 that also declared late impeachment unacceptable. The Florida Supreme Court held that:

> officers are officers; ex-officers, who could not be suspended or removed from office, are not. The court thus was making the linguistic argument that "officer" meant "sitting officer" and the functional argument that "the primary and dominant purpose of impeachment in Florida is removal of an officeholder from office. Once an officer has resigned, this purpose is fulfilled, the court said, and the mere possibility of disqualification from future office does not change the fact that the main purpose of the process has been achieved. The court considered Blount, Belknap, and Ferguson, but argued that in each case the resignation did not occur until impeachment proceedings had begun.[78]

B. Congress' Power To Impose Penalties Upon Conviction Of Impeachment Is Limited to Removal, And (Not Or) Disqualification.

The Constitution grants Congress only the power to remove a person's right to run for office when it is part of the process of removal from office. Article II, Section 4, of the Constitution states that the only purpose of an impeachment is whether "the President, Vice president and all civil Officers of the United States, shall be removed from office." The only purpose of impeachment is to remove the President, Vice-President, and civil officers from office. When a President is no longer in office, the objective of an impeachment ceases.[79]

---

77 *Smith v. Brantley*, 400 So. 2d 443 (Fla. 1981)

78 Kalt at 120-121.

79 Kalt at 66, *see also* fn. 112:

> *See, e.g.*, 14 Annals of Cong. 430-31 (1805) (speech of Luther Martin in impeachment trial of Justice Samuel Chase) ("The President, Vice President, and other civil officers can only be impeached.... In the first article, section the third, of the Constitution, it is declared that, judgment in all cases of impeachment, shall not extend further than removal from office, and disqualification to hold any office of honor, trust, or profit,

This impeachment trial is being pursued solely to preclude Mr. Trump, a private citizen, from holding any future office. However, the Constitution does not provide for the impeachment of a private citizen who is not in office. Further, the Constitution only grants the Senate the additional power to remove a person's right to run for office as *part* of the process of removal from office.[80] When a person ceases to hold an office, he immediately becomes a private citizen, impervious to removal, and therefore to impeachment and trial by the Senate.

As Professor Harold Krent has noted, "although the Impeachment Clause in Article I states that the penalty for impeachment shall not extend beyond removal and disqualification from office, that clause reads as a limit on what type of punishment can be meted rather than addressing "when." The Framers presumably were signaling the change from the British practice under which additional penalties were possible. There is no language in the Constitution suggesting that the impeachment authority is continuous."[81]

This idea was perhaps best expressed by Supreme Court Justice Joseph Story, in his influential three volume treatise *Commentaries on the Constitution of the United States*:

> **§ 801.** As it is declared in one clause of the constitution, that "judgment, in cases of impeachment, shall not extend further, than a removal from office, and disqualification to hold any office of honour, trust, or profit, under the United States;" and in another clause, that "the president, vice president, and all civil officers of the United States, shall be removed from office on impeachment for, and conviction of, treason, bribery, or other high crimes or misdemeanors;" it would seem to follow, that the senate, on the

under the United States. This clearly evinces, that no persons but those who hold offices are liable to impeachment.

[80] Dershowitz, *No, You can't try an Impeached Former President,* Wall Street Journal (Jan. 21, 2021),*https://www.wsj.com/articles/no-you-cant-try-an-impeached-former-president-11611167113?mod=article_inline* (contrasting the word "and" with the word "or.")

[81] Harold J. Krent, *Can President Trump Be Impeached As Mr. Trump? Exploring the Temporal Dimension of Impeachments*, 95 Chi.-Kent L. Rev. 537, 542 (2020).

> conviction, were bound, in all cases, to enter a judgment of removal from office, though it has a discretion, as to inflicting the punishment of disqualification. If, then, there must be a judgment of removal from office, it would seem to follow, that the constitution contemplated, that the party was still in office at the time of the impeachment. If he was not, his offence was still liable to be tried and punished in the ordinary tribunals of justice. And it might be argued with some force, that it would be a vain exercise of authority to try a delinquent for an impeachable offence, when the most important object, for which the remedy was given, was no longer necessary, or attainable. And although a judgment of disqualification might still be pronounced, the language of the constitution may create some doubt, whether it can be pronounced without being coupled with a removal from office.[82]

The House Managers' failure to grasp this concept is evident from their misplaced reliance on this language to try and create a work-around of a problem of their own making, i.e. Mr. Trump was no longer President at the time the House filed the Article of Impeachment in the Senate. Instead, their argument further demonstrates the point that Mr. Trump could not be removed from office (because his term ended), the condition precedent to any further penalty. As Professor Alan Dershowitz explained:

> The Constitution is clear: "The president . . . shall be removed from office on impeachment . . . and conviction"—not by the expiration of his term before the impeachment process is complete. It also mandates that "judgment in cases of impeachment shall not extend further than to removal and disqualification"—not *or* disqualification.[83]

[82] Justice Joseph Story, *Commentaries on the Constitution of the United States* at § 801.

[83] Alan Dershowitz, *No, You can't try an Impeached Former President,* Wall Street Journal, (Jan. 21, 2021), https://www.wsj.com/articles/no-you-cant-try-an-impeached-former-president-11611167113?mod=article_inline

Other scholars have forcefully rejected the failed interpretation the House Managers try to advance in an effort to salvage this doomed impeachment by spelling out the unstated assumptions inherent in their position:

> by this logic a president could be disqualified from holding office without being removed, an obvious absurdity. This argument asserts that, because the Senate could, by a simple majority, disqualify a person impeached and convicted under Article II, it would thwart the operation of Article I, Clause 7's list of permissible punishments to let the convicted former officer go free. Were it otherwise, an officer could avoid removal and disqualification by simply resigning. This circular argument assumes the truth of the proposition that a person no longer in office can be impeached in the first place and then infers from this assumption that such a power should not be frustrated. It is not compatible with Article II, which provides the sole constitutional grounds for trial in the Senate on the basis of which impeachment penalties can be imposed: the commission of bribery, treason, or other high crimes and misdemeanors by a civil officer leading to his removal. It relies instead on a tortured inference from Article I, whose text says nothing about who can be impeached or on what grounds. In an effort to salvage the penalty of disqualification where an official has been impeached while in office but has resigned, advocates for this view would have the Senate convict a person no longer in office, inventing a new basis for conviction beyond that provided in Article II.[84]

The Constitution does not provide for an impeachment of someone who is not in office as a means to an end resulting in only disqualification – and for good reason. As Alexander Hamilton wrote:

> Nothing is more common than for a free people, in times of heat and violence, to gratify momentary passions by letting into the government principles and precedents which afterwards prove fatal to themselves. Of this kind is the doctrine of disqualification, disfranchisement, and banishment by acts of the legislature. The dangerous consequences of this power are manifest. If the legislature can disfranchise any number of citizens at pleasure by general descriptions, it may soon confine all the votes to a small number of partisans, and establish an aristocracy or an oligarchy; if it may banish at discretion all those whom particular circumstances

---

84 Bobbit, *supra.*, https://www.lawfareblog.com/why-senate-shouldnt-hold-late-impeachment-trial

> render obnoxious, without hearing or trial, no man can be safe, nor know when he may be the innocent victim of a prevailing faction. The name of liberty applied to such a government would be a mockery of common sense.[85]

The House Managers put a lot of misplaced importance onto the fact that Article I Section 7 contains a clause reminding Congress of its own limitations, namely that after a conviction and removal, the only other penalty Congress can impose is disqualification. "Judgment in Cases of Impeachment shall not extend further than to removal from Office, and disqualification to hold and enjoy any Office of honor," does *not* mean that disqualification is a separate or alternative form of punishment entirely. Disqualification from future office is simply an additional discretionary penalty that the Senate may impose once it has determined the original purpose of the impeachment, removal, is proper. Disqualification, however, is not the purpose of an impeachment proceeding, and it is not available simply to disqualify a former public officer from future officeholding.

But that is not all. The House Managers are not content to argue that an officer who is impeached while in office can then be tried after they leave office;[86] the House Managers dig in further and claim that a person can be impeached at any time after they leave office.[87] The absence of a statute of limitations suggests that process is confined to present office holders: "A federal

---

85 Hamilton, A., *A Letter from Phocion to the Considerate Citizens of New York* (January 27, 1784), https://founders.archives.gov/documents/Hamilton/01-03-02-0314#ARHN-01-03-02-0314-fn-0001 .

86 Although the same textual inferences against such proceedings would apply, especially because there *were* states that *did* allow for just that: some states, there is an arguable textual and structural basis for drawing a distinction between the stages of impeachment. For instance, Nebraska state law provided: "An impeachment of any state officer shall be tried, notwithstanding such officer may have resigned his office, or his term of office has expired." This language more easily supports the notion that impeachment is limited to sitting officers but that trial is not. Kalt at 76 citing to *State v. Hill*, 55 N.W. at 798 (quoting Neb. Comp. Stat. ch. 19, § 8 (1891)).

87 House Trial Memo at 2.

cause of action 'brought at any distance of time' would be 'utterly repugnant to the genius of our laws.'"[88]

In addition, at any given moment in time "[t]he majority party could threaten to impeach former officeholders of the minority party unless support is forthcoming on a particular appropriations or other bill. In other words, the ongoing threat of impeachment might distort law-making... and, as a functional matter, might interfere with the balance of powers otherwise prescribed in the Constitution."[89]

This is a dangerous slippery slope that the Senate should be careful to avoid. Were it otherwise, a future House could impeach former Vice President Biden for his obstruction of justice in setting up the Russia hoax circa 2016. While he could not be removed from the Vice Presidency because his term ended in 2017, he could be barred from holding future office. The same flawed logic the House Managers advance could apply to former Secretary of State Clinton for her violations of 18 U.S.C § 793. Impeachment cannot and should not be allowed to devolve into a political weapon.

Setting aside the clear meaning of the text, the House Managers argument about the need for late impeachment with disqualification upon conviction to serve as a deterrence for Presidential wrongdoing is also unfounded. A President who left office is not in any way above the law; as the Constitution states he or she is like any other citizen and can be tried in a court of law. From a political standpoint as well, an officer who has left office and is seeking to return faces the *ultimate*

---

88 *Wilson v. Garcia*, 471 U.S. 261, 271, 105 S. Ct. 1938, 1944 (1985) (quoting *Adams v. Woods*, 6 U.S. (2 Cranch) 336, 342 (1805)), abrogated in part on other grounds, Pub. L. No. 101-650, Title III, § 313(a), 104 Stat. 5089, 5114-5115 (1990).

89 *Id. See also*, Laurent Sacharoff, *Former Presidents and Executive Privilege*, 88 Tex. L. Rev. 301, 315 (2009), noting that Congress "cannot impeach a former President."

political check even without disqualification- the electorate. It is almost laughable that the House Managers, who spent four years pretending that Mr. Trump was completely ineffective and illegitimate, are now so worried that he might win again that they seek to illegally impair him.

Accordingly, the Senate does not have the power to try a former President and should dismiss the Article of Impeachment. Any other outcome would do profound and lasting damage to the institution of the Presidency. In this political climate we have seen the statues and monuments of former Presidents attacked because the values of their times were not in line with supposed modern sensibilities; if this impeachment of a former President is allowed to go forward, we could expect dozens more to follow from potentially both sides of the aisle, depending on which party happens to be in the majority.

> Future Congresses would judge the conduct of Presidents and other civil officers from the perspective of a different political and social milieu. From the vantage point of subsequent Congresses, President Clinton may have had a #MeToo problem; President Lyndon Johnson evidently spoke disparagingly about race; President George W. Bush lied to the public about domestic surveillance, and so on. And, although historical judgment may, at times, be healthy, the power of impeachment comes with tangible penalties.[90]

It is also true that, even if the Senate were to convict him without jurisdiction, such a decision would not go unchallenged. If Mr. Trump decides to run again, any non-binding 'disqualification' from an unauthorized Senate vote could and would be challenged in a court of law.[91] As scholars across the spectrum have agreed, certain aspects of impeachment *are* justiciable.

---

[90] Harold J. Krent, *Can President Trump Be Impeached As Mr. Trump? Exploring the Temporal Dimension of Impeachments*, 95 Chi.-Kent L. Rev. 537, 546 (2020).

[91] Christopher Silvester, *Beware the bill of attainder*, The Critic (Jan. 29, 2021), https://thecritic.co.uk/beware-the-bill-of-attainder/

For example, if, in a case like this, where "the President was tried by someone other than the Chief Justice,"[92] a Court would be likely to hear the matter on review.[93]

C. The Article of Impeachment Violates Mr. Trump's First Amendment Rights

Aside from the fact that it does not constitute a crime, let alone a high crime or misdemeanor, President Trump's speech at the January 6, 2021 event fell well within the norms of political speech that is protected by the First Amendment, and to try him for that would be to

---

92 Josh Blackman, *What happens if the Chief Justice cannot serve at the Presidential impeachment trial?*, The Volokh Conspiracy (Nov. 25, 2019), https://reason.com/volokh/2019/11/25/what-happens-if-the-chief-justice-cannot-serve-at-the-presidential-impeachment-trial/.

93 As Adam Liptak described it in the NY Times;

> Still, the 1993 decision did appear to leave open a possible role for the court were the Senate to violate what Chief Justice Rehnquist wrote were "the three very specific requirements" in the constitutional text — "that the Senate's members must be under oath or affirmation, that a two-thirds vote is required to convict and that the chief justice presides when the president is tried."
> When the case was argued, he asked the government's lawyer, Solicitor General Ken Starr, whether violations of those provisions could be challenged in court. (Mr. Starr would go on to investigate Mr. Clinton as independent counsel and to prepare the report that led to his impeachment.)
> **For instance, Chief Justice Rehnquist asked, what would happen if the chief justice died and Congress "created the office of vice chief justice?"**
> "We're going to let him preside," the chief justice said, sketching out the Senate's reasoning, "because it would just be catastrophic to wait for the appointment of a chief justice while this impeachment is pending."
> "Can the Senate not do that because of the specific language 'the chief justice shall preside'?" Chief Justice Rehnquist asked. "Would that action by the Senate, followed by the presiding by the vice chief justice, be judicially reviewable?"
> "I have to admit," Mr. Starr said, with apparent reluctance, that the answer was yes.

Adam Liptak, *Can Trump Challenge His Impeachment in the Supreme Court*, New York Times (Dec. 17, 2019), https://www.nytimes.com/2019/11/25/us/trump-impeachment-supreme-court.html.

do a grave injustice to the freedom of speech in this country.[94] Perhaps in realization that Mr. Trump's speech was clearly within the bounds the protections afforded by the First Amendment, the House Managers attempt to erect artificial roadblocks to prevent the Senate from even considering First Amendment principles in these impeachment proceedings. These efforts – as fully discussed below – are complete sophistry that should be rejected by the Senators, who are duty bound to consider and apply the First Amendment.

1. The Senate Cannot Disregard the First Amendment and the Supreme Court's Long-Established Free Speech Jurisprudence

The House Managers' Trial Memorandum expressly advocates for the Senate to disregard First Amendment principles, stating "the First Amendment does not apply *at all* to an impeachment proceeding."[95] In doing so, the House Managers shockingly invite Senators to violate their own oaths to uphold the Constitution and the bedrock principle—established over two hundred years ago—that the Supreme Court is the final arbiter of whether Congressional acts are consistent with the Constitution.[96] There is no actual precedent for this confounding precept offered in the House Managers' Brief—the Managers astonishingly cite to a few recent internet *blogs*.[97]

The First Amendment is widely understood as prohibiting Congress from "abridging the freedom of speech; or the right of people peaceably to assemble" in all aspects of state action in

---

94 Miranda Devine, *Facebook's squad of though police: Devine*, https://nypost.com/2021/01/31/facebooks-squad-of-thought-police-devine/; *see also* Tammy Bruce, *The new thought police: Inside the left's assault on free speech and free minds* (Crown, 2010).

95 House Trial Memo. at 45.

96 *Marbury v. Madison*, 5 U.S. 137 (1803) ("It is emphatically the province and duty of the Judicial Department to say what the law is.")

97 Mem. of U.S. House of Rep. at 45 n.201.

all three branches of government.[98] Congress may not take action that would "abridge the freedom of speech." Indeed, Senators take an Oath of Office, which includes an oath to "support and defend the Constitution of the United States . . . ."[99] The Constitution, of course, includes the Bill of Rights, including the First Amendment. This means, inevitably, that Senators cannot do what the House Managers urge: the Senate cannot blithely cast aside the First Amendment and the Supreme Court's long-established Free Speech jurisprudence when passing judgment on articles of impeachment.

The Constitution must, at a minimum, serve as a limitation on the ability of Congress to impeach for "high crimes and misdemeanors." As noted by a Constitutional scholar a few years ago, if that were not the case, there would be a host of internal contradictions within the Constitution that could not have been intended by the Framers:

> Additional *negative* restrictions would also extend from the panoply of protections in the Bill of Rights. For example, an officer could not be removed from office for refusing to self-incriminate (Fifth Amendment) or seeking the assistance of counsel in a criminal prosecution (Sixth Amendment). Whatever "high crimes and Misdemeanors" means, it cannot include conduct that is itself protected by the Constitution; such would be an internal contradiction. Or, to frame it in modern doctrine, it would amount

---

98 While the First Amendment explicitly states that "Congress shall make no laws" abridging freedom of speech or of the press, by settled tradition it "has been read to apply to the entire national government." U.S. Constitution, 1st Am.; Gerald Gunther, *Constitutional Law, Cases and Materials* 462 (10th ed. 1982); *Valley Forge Christian Coll. v. Americans United for Separation of Church & State, Inc.*, 454 U.S. 464, 511 (1982) (Brennan, J. dissenting on other grounds) ("The First Amendment binds the Government as a whole, regardless of which branch is at work in a particular instance."); *Richmond Newspapers*, 448 U.S. at 575 ("The First Amendment . . . prohibits governments from 'abridging the freedom of speech, or of the press."); *Smith v. California*, 361 U.S. 147, 157 (1960) (Black, J., concurring) ("The First Amendment . . . fixed its own value on freedom of speech and press by putting these freedoms wholly 'beyond the reach' of federal power to abridge.").

99 U.S. Senate Website, *Oath of Office*, https://www.senate.gov/artandhistory/history/common/briefing/Oath_Office.htm

> to an unconstitutional condition: punishing a person for exercising a right protected by the Constitution.[100]

The position advanced by the House Managers is essentially an impeachment standard without Constitutional guardrails, unmoored to any specific legal test other than the unbridled whims of the House Managers. That distinctly was not what the Framers intended when they expressly limited impeachable offenses to "high crimes and misdemeanors." The Framers of the Constitution were keenly aware of the danger of any impeachment process that would make the President "the mere creature of the Legislature."[101] Such an arrangement would constitute nothing less than "a violation of the fundamental principle of good Government."[102]

Founding Father James Wilson, who was a renowned legal scholar, served as one of the six initial Supreme Court Justices (1789-1798), and was a major force in drafting the Constitution,[103] plainly stated in his law lectures that lawful and constitutional conduct may not be used as an impeachable offense:

> The doctrine of impeachments is of high import in the constitutions of free states. On one hand, the most powerful magistrates should be amenable to the law: on the other hand, elevated characters should not be sacrificed merely on account of their elevation. No

---

100 Josh Blackman, *Obstruction of Justice and the Presidency: Part II*, Lawfare (Dec. 12, 2017)(emphasis original), https://www.lawfareblog.com/obstruction-justice-and-presidency-part-i.

101 2 *Records of the Federal Convention of 1787*, at 86 (Max Farrand ed., rev. ed. 1937).

102 *Id.*

103 "James Wilson (September 14, 1742 – August 21, 1798) was an American statesmen, politician, legal scholar, and Founding Father who served as an Associate Justice of the United States Supreme Court from 1789 to 1798. He was elected twice to the Continental Congress, was a signatory of the United States Declaration of Independence, and was a major force in drafting the United States Constitution. A leading legal theorist, he was one of the six original justices appointed by George Washington to the Supreme Court of the United States. In his capacity as first Professor of Law at the University of Pennsylvania, he taught the first course on the new Constitution to President Washington and his cabinet in 1789 and 1790." https://en.wikipedia.org/wiki/James_Wilson_(founding_father)

> one should be secure while he violates the constitution and the laws: ***everyone should be secure while he observes them*.**[104]

The House Managers' suggestion that the First Amendment does not apply to this impeachment process is untenable. It conflicts with common sense, the Senators' Oath of Office, well-settled Supreme Court precedent, and the intent of the Framers of the Constitution, such as James Wilson, who not only was a draftsman of the Constitution, but taught the first course on the new Constitution to President Washington and his cabinet in Philadelphia at the University of Pennsylvania in 1789. The Senate should soundly reject the Managers' invitation to disregard the Constitution.

2. Mr. Trump as an Elected Official Has First Amendment Rights to Freely Engage in Political Speech

Another roadblock the House Managers use is the legally unsupported idea that because Mr. Trump was an elected official, specifically the President, he has fewer rights under the First Amendment than everyone else in the United States. This, too, is sophistry. The opposite is true. The Supreme Court of the United States has long held that the First Amendment's right to freedom of speech protects elected officials such as Mr. Trump. The House Managers' argument to the contrary both ignores well-established precedent and erodes the constitutional principles guiding this august body. In fact, the argument of the House Managers so materially omits the relevant constitutional precepts that an extended discussion becomes both necessary and warranted, particularly in light of the public commentary relied upon in the House Trial Memorandum.

There can be no dispute that elected public officials engage in protected free speech when they speak out on investigations of voting regularity and fairness. The Supreme Court held that an elected sheriff who spoke out on an investigation of voting patterns, and even communicated

---

104 *Collected Works of James Wilson,* Vol. 2 at 861 (Hall Kermit ed., 2007).

with a sitting grand jury via open letter, was protected by the First Amendment from punitive action by another group of "elected officers" for "publishing views honestly held and contrary to those" advocated by his accusers in the other political party.[105] Justice Brennan, writing for the majority in *Wood v. Georgia*, went so far as to make the protection of an elected public official a core First Amendment principle because the voting controversy at issue directly affected the sheriff's political career:

> The petitioner was an elected official and had the right to enter the field of political controversy, particularly where his political life was at stake. The role that elected officials play in our society makes it all the more imperative that they be allowed freely to express themselves on matters of current public importance.[106]

To paraphrase *Wood*, if Mr. Trump could be silenced in this manner by Congress, the Constitutional problem becomes evident: [107] a difference of political opinion, expressed in speech, on an issue of voting irregularity cannot be punishable where all that was done was to encourage investigation of voting irregularities and peaceful political speech.[108]

If *Wood* alone was not dispositive of Mr. Trump's free speech rights as an elected official to address public controversies such as voting irregularities and the authority of officials certifying votes, the Supreme Court emphatically held shortly after *Wood* that a legislature cannot punish an elected official for protected political speech. *Bond v. Floyd* squarely addresses the question of an

---

105 *Wood v. Georgia*, 370 U.S. 375, 390–91, 394-95 (1962).

106 *Wood*, 370 U.S. at 394-95 (citation and footnote omitted).

107 *Id.* at 390-91.

108 "I know that everyone here will soon be marching over to the Capitol building to peacefully and patriotically make your voices heard." Transcript of January 6, 2021 Speech at approximately 18:16, available at https://www.rev.com/blog/transcripts/donald-trump-speech-save-america-rally-transcript-january-6.

elected official's punishment by a legislature for statements alleged to have incited public violation of the law, unequivocally rejecting the idea that an elected official is entitled to lesser, or no, protection under the First Amendment. When the state argued "that even though such a citizen might be protected by his First Amendment rights, the State may nonetheless apply a stricter standard to its legislators[,]" the Supreme Court responded tersely, "We do not agree[,]" and held the action of the legislature against the elected official unconstitutional and in violation of his First Amendment rights.[109]

The *Bond* case is particularly instructive, because the petitioner opposed the Vietnam war draft, and was accused of endorsing the burning of draft cards—a position he subsequently clarified, noting that he possessed his own draft card and did not support burning draft cards.[110] As punishment for articulating this position in theoretical conflict with federal law, the Georgia House of Representatives to which he was elected refused to seat him—a purely legislative action, like impeachment.[111] Based in part upon Bond's subsequent clarification that he did not urge anyone to burn draft cards, the Supreme Court first concluded that Bond "could not have been constitutionally convicted under 50 U.S.C. App. s 462(a), which punishes any person who 'counsels, aids, or abets another to refuse or evade registration.'"[112]

Going further, the Supreme Court held that the Georgia House of Representatives was in fact forbidden by the First Amendment from punishing Bond for advocating against the policy of the United States. It began by once again rejecting outright the argument that an elected official

---

109 *Bond v. Floyd*, 385 U.S. 116, 132–33 (1966).

110 *Bond*, 385 U.S. at 118-25 ("I have not counselled burning draft cards, nor have I burned mine.")

111 *Id.* at 125.

112 *Id.* at 133-34.

could be held to any "higher standard" or that the Georgia House could "limit[] its legislators' capacity to discuss their views of local or national policy."[113] Justice Brennan, once again writing for the majority, went on to reaffirm the Constitutional shield around the speech of elected officials, even extending it to statements deemed "erroneous:"

> The manifest function of the First Amendment in a representative government requires that legislators be given the widest latitude to express their views on issues of policy. The central commitment of the First Amendment, as summarized in the opinion of the Court in *New York Times v. Sullivan*, 376 U.S. 254, 270, 84 S.Ct. 710, 721, 11 L.Ed.2d 686 (1964), is that 'debate on public issues should be uninhibited, robust, and wide-open.' We think the rationale of the *New York Times* case disposes of the claim that Bond's statements fell outside the range of constitutional protection. Just as erroneous statements must be protected to give freedom of expression the breathing space it needs to survive, so statements criticizing public policy and the implementation of it must be similarly protected. The State argues that the *New York Times* principle should not be extended to statements by a legislator because the policy of encouraging free debate about governmental operations only applies to the citizen-critic of his government. We find no support for this distinction in the *New York Times* case or in any other decision of this Court. The interest of the public in hearing all sides of a public issue is hardly advanced by extending more protection to citizen-critics than to legislators. Legislators have an obligation to take positions on controversial political questions so that their constituents can be fully informed by them, and be better able to assess their qualifications for office; also so they may be represented in governmental debates by the person they have elected to represent them.[114]

Mr. Trump's statements and advocacy of his political opinions—abhorred by the opponents of freedom of speech in the House as they may be—is no less protected than Bond's speech. Mr. Trump, having been elected nationally, was elected to be the voice for his national

---

[113] *Id.* at 135.

[114] *Id.* at 135-37.

constituency. It is undeniable that the First Amendment's protections flow to him as an elected official where he was, as Wood, addressing the electoral integrity issues essential to his career that he has consistently advocated, a position unpopular with his political opponents. Furthermore, as Mr. Trump expressly urged rally participants "to peacefully and patriotically make your voices heard"[115] on January 6, 2021, his political speech falls squarely within the protections of the First Amendment under clear Supreme Court precedent (as fully discussed below), and he thus cannot be convicted by a Senate sworn to uphold the Constitution.

Contrary to these express holdings of the Supreme Court, as announced more than fifty years ago, the House Managers assert in their memorandum that "the First Amendment does not shield public officials who occupy sensitive policymaking positions from adverse actions when their speech undermines important government interests."[116] In making this spurious claim, the Managers rely on two cases concerning *appointed* public employees,[117] having inexplicably failed to bring to the Senate's attention the squarely and obviously on-point Supreme Court authority concerning *elected* public officials (discussed at length *supra*).

The House Manager's two cases, however, address the wholly different situation of public defenders and sheriff's office employees suffering unconstitutional dismissals based on party affiliation. Those individuals were protected from employment termination—not impeachment—because they were not policy-makers or possessors of confidential information, and thus, their

---

115 Transcript of January 6, 2021 Speech at approximately 18:16, available at https://www.rev.com/blog/transcripts/donald-trump-speech-save-america-rally-transcript-january-6.

116 House Trial Memo. at 46.

117 *Branti v. Finkel*, 445 U.S. 507 (1980); *Elrod v. Burns*, 427 U.S. 347 (1976).

"private political beliefs" could not interfere with their duties.[118] Such cases cannot serve as the basis for a First Amendment analysis of Mr. Trump, or in fact any president, because elected officials are different in kind from non-elected public employees under the First Amendment.

The Supreme Court, in fact, expressly rejected the House Managers' First Amendment argument when confronting the voting investigation speech at issue in *Wood*.[119] Justice Brennan examined the line of cases addressing termination of non-elected public employees and found it inapplicable to the case of the elected sheriff:

> Petitioner was not a civil servant, but an elected official, and hence this is not a case like *United Public Workers v. Mitchell*, 330 U.S. 75, 67 S.Ct. 556, 91 L.Ed. 754, in which this Court held that congress has the power to circumscribe the political activities of federal employees in the career public service.

As *Mitchell* was the case relied upon in *Elrod*[120] and *Branti*,[121] and its factual predicate was expressly rejected as a basis for evaluation of an elected public official's First Amendment rights in *Wood*, the House Managers have built their case against the First Amendment upon the proverbial foundation of sand, and have no support for their argument that Mr. Trump lacks protection under the First Amendment as all Supreme Court authority is directly contrary to their assertions.

---

118 *Branti*, 445 U.S. at 517 (synthesizing rule in *Elrod*).

119 *Wood*, 370 U.S. at 395 n.21.

120 427 U.S. at 357, 362, 366-70.

121 445 U.S. at 515 n.10.

3. Mr. Trump's Speech Was Fully Protected by the First Amendment

Mr. Trump engaged in constitutionally protected political speech that the House has, improperly, characterized as "incitement of insurrection." The attempt of the House to transmute Mr. Trump's speech—core free speech under the First Amendment—into an impeachable offense cannot be supported, and convicting him would violate the very Constitution the Senate swears to uphold.

House Resolution 24 contains only one article of impeachment: incitement of insurrection.[122] The allegations made i that article are that Mr. Trump engaged in speech of various kinds concerning a public, political event: the Presidential election of November 2020. Specifically, House Resolution 24 focuses upon Mr. Trump's speech on January 6, 2021.[123] The article also discusses in passing other "statements" of Mr. Trump as well as a telephone call to the secretary of state of Georgia.[124]

The fatal flaw of the House's arguments is that it seeks to mete out governmental punishment – impeachment—based on political speech that falls squarely within broad protections of the First Amendment. Speech and association for political purposes is the kind of activity to which the First Amendment offers its strongest protection.[125] Restrictions placed on freedom of

---

122 H. Res. 24 at 2, 117th Cong. (Jan. 11, 2021). The sole article of impeachment is framed under the "high Crimes and Misdemeanors" clause of Article II, and does not allege treason or bribery. U.S. CONST. art. II, § 4.

123 *Id.* at 2-3.

124 *Id.* at 2, 4.

125 *New York Times Co. v.* Sullivan, 376 U.S. 254, 269 (1964)(The First Amendment "'was fashioned to assure unfettered interchange of ideas for the bringing about of political and social changes desired by the people.'" (quoting *Roth v. United States,* 354 U.S. 476, 484 (1957)).

speech are evaluated "against the background of a profound national commitment to the principle that debate on public issues should be uninhibited, robust, and wide open, and that it may well include vehement, caustic, and sometimes unpleasantly sharp attacks on government and public officials."[126] Thus, "[o]ur First Amendment decisions have created a rough hierarchy in the constitutional protection of speech" in which "[c]ore political speech occupies the highest, most protected position."[127]

The Supreme Court has further acknowledged that "[t]he language of the political arena . . . is often vituperative, abusive, and inexact."[128] A rule of law permitting criminal or civil liability to be imposed upon those who speak or write on public issues and their superintendence would lead to "self-censorship" by all which would not be relieved by permitting a defense of truth. "Under such a rule, would-be critics of official conduct may be deterred from voicing their criticism, even though it is believed to be true and even though it is in fact true, because of doubt whether it can be proved in court or fear of the expense of having to do so . . . . The rule thus dampens the vigor and limits the variety of public debate."[129] In only a few well defined and

---

126 *Watts v. United States*, 394 U.S. 705, 708 (1969) (quoting *New York Times Co. v. Sullivan*, 376 U.S. 254, 270 (1964)).

127 *R.A.V. v. St. Paul*, 505 U.S. 377, 422 (1992(Stevens, J., concurring); *see also Hill v. Colorado*, 530 U.S. 703, 787 (2000)(Kennedy, J., dissenting)("Laws punishing speech which protests the lawfulness or morality of the government's own policy are the essence of the tyrannical power the First Amendment guards against."); *Citizens United v. Federal Election Comm'n*, 588 U.S. 310, 349 (2010)("If the First Amendment has any force, it prohibits Congress from fining or jailing citizens, or associations of citizens, for simply engaging in political speech.")

128 *Watts*, 394 U.S. at 708 (distinguishing between "political hyperbole" and "true threats") (citing *Linn v. United Plant Guard Workers of America*, 383 U.S. 53, 58, (1966)).

129 *New York Times*, 376 U.S. at 279.

narrowly limited classes of speech may the government punish an individual for his or her words.[130]

Even political speech that *may* incite unlawful conduct is protected from the reach of governmental punishment. Indeed, "[e]very idea is an incitement,' and if speech may be suppressed whenever it *might* inspire someone to act unlawfully, then there is no limit to the State's censorial power."[131] The government may not prohibit speech because it increases the chance an unlawful act will be committed "at some indefinite future time."[132] Rather, the government may *only* suppress speech for advocating the use of force or a violation of law if **"such advocacy is directed to inciting or producing imminent lawless action and is likely to incite or produce such action."[133]**

In *Brandenburg v. Ohio*, the Supreme Court formed a test that placed even speech inciting illegal conduct within the protection of the First Amendment.[134] In that case, a leader of the Ku Klux Klan was convicted under an Ohio criminal syndicalism law.[135] Evidence of his incitement was a film of the events at a Klan rally, which included racist and anti-Semitic speech, the burning of a large wooden cross, and several items that appeared in the film, including a number of

---

130 *Gooding v. Wilson*, 405 U.S. 518, 521-22 (1972).

131 *Lorillard Tobacco Co. v. Reilly*, 533 U.S. 525, 580, 121 S.Ct. 2404, 2435, 150 L.Ed.2d 532 (2001)(emphasis added)(quoting *Gitlow v. New York*, 268 U.S. 652, 673, 45 S.Ct. 625, 69 L.Ed. 1138 (1925)(Holmes, J., dissenting)).

132 *Ashcroft v. Free Speech Coal.*, 535 U.S. 234, 253–54 (2002)(quoting *Hess v. Indiana*, 414 U.S. 105, 108 (1973)(*per curiam*)).

133 *Brandenburg v. Ohio*, 395 U.S. 444, 447 (1969) (emphasis added) (*per curiam*).

134 395 U.S. at 447.

135 *Id.* at 445.

firearms.[136] The leader of the protest proclaimed that "[w]e're not a revengent [sic] organization, but if our President, our Congress, our Supreme Court, continues to suppress the white, Caucasian race, it's possible that there might be some revenge taken. We are marching on Congress July the Fourth, four hundred thousand strong."[137] The Court held that, "the constitutional guarantees of free speech and free press do not permit [the government] to forbid or proscribe advocacy of the use of force or of law violation except where such advocacy is directed to inciting or producing imminent lawless action and is likely to incite or produce such action."[138] The Court explained that "the mere abstract teaching of the moral propriety or even moral necessity for a resort to force and violence, is not the same as preparing a group for violent action and steeling it to such action.[139]

Thus, under *Brandenburg* and its progeny, government actors may not "forbid or proscribe advocacy of the use of force or of law violation except where such advocacy is directed to inciting or producing imminent lawless action and is likely to incite or produce such action."[140] Absent an imminent threat, therefore, it is expressly within the First Amendment to advocate for the use of force; similarly, it is protected speech to advocate for violating the law; and as Mr. Trump did neither of these things, his speech at all times fell well within First Amendment protections. He thus cannot be subject to conviction by the Senate under well-established First Amendment jurisprudence.

---

136 *Id.* at 445-46.

137 *Id.* at 446.

138 *Id.*

139 *Id.* at 448.

140 *Id.*

The article of impeachment cherry picks Mr. Trump's phrases from an hour-long speech, and indeed other speeches before other audiences, but even looked at through the lens of House Resolution 24, the incitement alleged is sterile and thin. The House's case for "incitement" simply fails to pass constitutional muster.

First, Mr. Trump unambiguously advocated to the crowd at the January 6, 2021 event that he expected peaceful behavior. He explicitly stated, "I know that everyone here will soon be marching over to the Capitol building to ***peacefully*** and patriotically make your voices heard."[141] Indeed, after reports of violence at the Capitol Mr. Trump issued a public video statement, urging the crowd at the Capitol to "go home" in "peace" and further pleading:

> we have to have peace, we have to have law and order, we have to respect our great people in law and order, we don't want anyone hurt. . .[142]

Mr. Trump's explicit disavowal of violence and calls for peace – both directly before and after the riot – and his urge to have the participants use their "voices" as opposed to other action cannot be ignored. Given these express statements, and the fact that the First Amendment protects elected public officials who disclaim violence or violations of the law,[143] the inquiry need go no further. Mr. Trump incited no insurrection, and his speech as a whole (despite all of the rhetoric

---

141 Transcript of January 6, 2021 Speech at approximately 18:16 (emphasis added), available at https://www.rev.com/blog/transcripts/donald-trump-speech-save-america-rally-transcript-january-6.

142 Video Starting at :22, located at https://www.c-span.org/video/?507774-1/president-trump-claims-election-stolen-tells-protesters-leave-capitol.

143 *Bond*, 385 U.S. at 125, 133-34 ("I have not counselled burning draft cards, nor have I burned mine.").

in House Resolution 24) cannot support a conviction because the First Amendment protected him at all times from government retribution.

Second, the House's heavy reliance on Mr. Trump's metaphorical "fighting" language is completely devoid of context, which, when considered as a whole, places Mr. Trump's speech entirely within the protection of the First Amendment. The thrust of the House's allegation against Mr. Trump is that he said, in the context of election security generally, that "if you don't ***fight*** like hell you're not going to have a country anymore."[144] To characterize this statement alone as "incitement to insurrection" is to ignore, wholesale, the remainder of Mr. Trump's speech that day, including his call for his supporters to "peacefully" making their "voices heard."

What is more, a closer examination of the text of Mr. Trump's speech reveals he makes references to "fighting" in a plainly figurative sense. For example, the metaphor of boxing permeated Mr. Trump's speech. He expressly referred to the sport in his speech, associating it with the word "fighting:" "Republicans are constantly ***fighting*** like a boxer with his hands tied behind his back. It's like a boxer[.]"[145] The House cannot seriously argue that Mr. Trump's use of the word "fighting" in this speech incited an insurrection, given this usage; it is not merely couched in the language of simile ("like") but it describes a position of physical disadvantage; it is far from a prescription for future violent action.

Mr. Trump used the word "fights" in the figurative sense of arguing, or putting forth an extreme effort, just as he did a short time later, speaking of Rep. Jordan:

---

144 H. Res. 24 at 3, 117th Cong. (Jan. 11, 2021).

145 Transcript of January 6, 2021 Speech at approximately 16:25 (emphasis added).

> There's so many weak Republicans. We have great ones, Jim Jordan, and some of these guys. They're out there ***fighting*** the House. Guys are ***fighting***, but it's incredible.[146]

Mr. Trump again used the word "fighting," but Rep. Jordan was not punching any of his fellow representatives. Mr. Trump referred to Rep. Jordan's *advocacy* efforts. This is entirely consistent with yet another use of the word, in reference to action at the ballot box, not violence:

> Unbelievable, what we have to go through, what we have to go through and you have to get your people to ***fight***. If they don't ***fight***, we have to primary the hell out of the ones that don't ***fight***. You primary them. We're going to let you know who they are. I can already tell you, frankly.[147]

Again, Mr. Trump used the word "fight" in the sense of forceful argument, and combined it with a plainly nonviolent request: he sought a change in the occupants of Congress through future primary elections, not through violence.

None of this constituted anything from which a conviction may follow: Mr. Trump's speech on January 6, 2021 was protected political speech, that which receives the strongest protection under the First Amendment, when the protections of free speech are at their highest.[148] In fact, under *Brandenburg*, there is no doubt that the words upon which the article of impeachment issued could never support a conviction, as there was plainly no advocacy of "lawless action" and the words, as stated, can hardly be interpreted to be "likely" to "incite imminent" violence or lawless action.

---

146 *Id.* at approximately 12:34 (emphasis added).

147 *Id.* at approximately 13:45 (emphasis added).

148 *Arizona Free Enter. Club's Freedom Club PAC v. Bennett*, 564 U.S. 721, 734 (2011).

Neither can the other allegations in the article of impeachment support a conviction given Mr. Trump's plain and clear First Amendment protection. The allegations of other "statements" alleged to contribute to an "incitement of insurrection"[149] are bereft of detail, and even as expanded upon in the House Managers' Trial Memorandum, amount to no more than Mr. Trump's advocating his position that he won the Presidential election in November 2020.

The allegation that Mr. Trump should be convicted for "incitement of insurrection" based upon the telephone call to the Georgia secretary of state rests on even shakier ground. The allegations of "threats of death and violence" come not from Mr. Trump at all; they come from other individuals from the internet, not identified (nor identifiable) in the House Trial Memorandum, who took it upon themselves to make inane internet threats, which were not urged or "incited" by Mr. Trump in any way shape or form.[150] Examining the discussion with the Georgia secretary of state under the standard of "incitement," leads to the same conclusion as the January 6, 2021 statements of Mr. Trump: there is nothing said by Mr. Trump that urges "use of force" or "law violation" directed to producing imminent lawless action.[151]

Even the House Managers' sinister and selective summary of Mr. Trumps' call cannot meet the standard for "incitement:" the analysis of the Supreme Court in *Hess v. Indiana* makes this apparent.[152] The question is not, as the House Managers seek to frame it, whether Mr. Trump's call offends the House's sensibilities; it is whether the call—which is plainly political speech in

---

149 H. Res. 24 at 3, 117th Cong. (Jan. 11, 2021).

150 House Trial Memo. at 9-10.

151 *Brandenburg*, 395 U.S. at 447.

152 414 U.S. 105, 107-10 (1973).

the sense that *Woods* concerns political speech, no different than the sheriff's letter to the grand jurors[153]—is outside the First Amendment based on the limited classes of speech beyond its ambit.[154] Mr. Trump's call was not obscene, nor did it contain fighting words, nor incitement: it was a political call, and such political speech must receive the highest protection afforded under the First Amendment.

The events of January 6, 2021, at the Capitol were terrible. The loss of life of any citizen, let alone a member of the Capitol Police, is a tragedy, but impeaching a former President is not the answer. The Senate should vote to clear Mr. Trump of any wrongdoing: "the hostile reaction of a crowd does not transform protected speech into incitement."[155] What matters is the objective meaning of the words. Courts do not deem speech unprotected based on how it could possibly be contorted or misunderstood by an unreasonable listener. Rather, they engage in an objective inquiry to determine how a reasonable person would understand the words. Otherwise, speakers at public events would be put at the mercy of the unhinged reactions of their most unreasonable audience members. That is exactly what happened on January 6th, but the Senate, composed of reasonable and erudite members, can take a few minutes and read the speech themselves.

In *Brandenburg*, the Supreme Court erected an extremely high bar to proving incitement.[156] That test requires proof that "(1) the speech explicitly or implicitly encouraged the use of violence or lawless action, (2) the speaker intends that his speech will result in the use of violence or lawless

---

153 *Wood*, 370 U.S. at 390–91, 394-95.

154 *Hess*, 414 U.S. at 107-08.

155 *Bible Believers v. Wayne Co.*, 805 F.3d 228, 246 (6th Cir. 2015).

156 *James v. Meow Media, Inc.*, 300 F.3d 683, 698 (6th Cir. 2002) (en banc).

action, and (3) the imminent use of violence or lawless action is the likely result of his speech."[157] The allegations against Mr. Trump unquestionably fail as a matter of law because "[a]dvocacy for the use of force or lawless behavior, intent, and imminence, are all absent." [158]Thus, "[t]he doctrine of incitement has absolutely no application" to this case. [159]

First, as evident from the transcript and the video of the speech in question, Mr. Trump's statements did not advocate—or even mention—the use of any force whatsoever. Because "[t]he mere tendency of speech to encourage unlawful acts is not a sufficient reason for banning it,"[160] it is all the more true that a statement that "fails to specifically advocate" for the crowd "to take 'any action' cannot constitute incitement."[161] Indeed, Mr. Trump expressly made a specific demand in his speech that all members of the audience - all protestors - behave "peacefully."

As the Sixth Circuit has recognized, "[i]t is not an easy task to find that speech rises to such a dangerous level that it can be deemed incitement to riot."[162] And unsurprisingly, "[t]here will rarely be enough evidence to create a jury question on whether a speaker was intending to incite imminent crime."[163] Consider *Hess v. Indiana*, where a protester yelled, "We'll take the fucking street again," to a crowd that was already agitated and resisting police.[164] The Court held

---

157 *Bible Believers v. Wayne Cty., Mich.*, 805 F.3d 228, 246 (6th Cir. 2015).

158 *Id.* at 244.

159 *Id.*

160 *Ashcroft v. Free Speech Coal.*, 535 U.S. 234, 253 (2002).

161 *Bible Believers*, 805 F.3d at 244 (quoting *Hess v. Indiana*, 414 U.S. 105, 109 (1973)).

162 *Id.*

163 Eugene Volokh, *Crime-Facilitating Speech*, 57 STAN. L. REV. 1095, 1190 (2005).

164 414 U.S. at 107.

that speech could not be punished.[165] Or take *NAACP v. Claiborne Hardware Co.*, where a speaker told a crowd that anyone who failed to boycott businesses would be "disciplined," and said, "If we catch any of you going in any of them racist stores, we're gonna break your damn neck."[166] The Court held that this speech was not incitement.[167] If these incendiary statements, with express references to violence, do not rise to the level of incitement, then surely Mr. Trump's request to peacefully protest could never be incitement.

In *Bible Believers*, the Court held the speech did not amount to incitement to riot under the *Brandenburg* test, despite the obviously explosive context, because it did not include "a single word" that could be perceived as encouraging, explicitly or implicitly, violence or lawlessness.[168] The same can be said of Mr. Trump's speech in this case: not a single word encouraged violence or lawlessness, explicitly or implicitly, and again, he affirmatively exhorted the crowd to act "peacefully" when protesting. Moreover, the *Bible Believers* court observed that "[t]he hostile reaction of a crowd does not transform protected speech into incitement."[169] Even though the Bible Believers' speech actually triggered a predictably violent reaction, it was their speech that the court scrutinized. And their speech was held to be protected, despite its blatantly offensive and even provocative nature and despite the crowd's reaction. It follows that if Mr. Trump's speech is protected—because it, like that of the Bible Believers, did not include a single word encouraging violence—then the fact that audience members reacted by using force does not transform Mr.

---

165 *Id.*

166 *NAACP v. Claiborne Hardware Co*, 458 U.S. 886, 902 (1982).

167 *Id.* at 928–29.

168 *Id.* at 246.

169 *Id.*

Trump's protected speech into unprotected speech. The reaction of listeners who may or may not be hostile does not alter the otherwise protected nature of speech.[170]

Nor is "the mere tendency of speech to encourage unlawful acts ... sufficient reason for banning it."[171] What is required, to forfeit constitutional protection, is incitement speech that "specifically advocate[s]" for listeners to take unlawful action.[172] Again, even assuming that then-President Trump's words may arguably have had a tendency to encourage unlawful use of force (which they did not), they certainly did not specifically advocate for listeners to take unlawful action and are therefore protected. As the *Bible Believers* court further observed, "[i]t is not an easy task to find that speech rises to such a dangerous level that it can be deemed incitement to riot."[173] The words alleged in the current case, much less offensive than those of the Bible Believers, are not up to the high standard demanded by *Brandenburg*.

Because not a single word of the speech actually advocates violence either implicitly or explicitly, the first *Brandenburg* factor—specific advocacy of violence— is totally absent. The allegations in the Article seems to place heavy reliance on the latter two *Brandenburg* factors. That is, the allegations that Mr. Trump intended violence to occur and knew that his words were likely to result in violence. But this backwards approach was specifically rejected in *Hess v. Indiana*, where the Court reversed the judgment of the Indiana Supreme Court.[174] In *Hess*, the Court noted that the state court had placed primary reliance on evidence that the speaker's

---

170 *Forsyth County, Georgia v. Nationalist Movement*, 505 U.S. 123 (1992).

171 *Ashcroft v. Free Speech Coal.*, 535 U.S. 234, 253, 122 S.Ct. 1389, 152 L.Ed.2d 403 (2002).

172 *Id.* (citing *Hess*, 414 U.S. at 109.

173 *Id.* at 244.

174 *Hess v. Indiana* 414 U.S. at 107–09.

statement was intended to incite further lawless action and was likely to produce such action. This was not enough. The *Hess* Court focused on the words, on the language, that comprised the subject speech, i.e., the first *Brandenburg* factor. "It hardly needs repeating," the Court repeated, "that the constitutional guarantees of freedom of speech forbid the States to punish the use of words or language not within narrowly limited classes of speech."[175] And in applying this wisdom, the Court likewise tied its conclusion to the words of the subject speech: "And since there was no evidence or rational inference from the import of the language, that his words were intended to produce, and likely to produce, imminent disorder, those words could not be punished by the State on the ground that they had 'a tendency to lead to violence.'"[176]

In other words, *Hess* teaches that the speaker's intent to encourage violence (second factor) and the tendency of his statement to result in violence (third factor) are not enough to forfeit First Amendment protection unless the words used specifically advocated the use of violence, whether explicitly or implicitly (first factor).

In *Snyder v. Phelps*, the Court observed: "[T]he court is obligated to make an independent examination of the whole record in order to make sure that the judgment does not constitute a forbidden intrusion on the field of free expression. In considering content, form, and context, no factor is dispositive, and it is necessary to evaluate all the circumstances of the speech, including what was said, where it was said, and how it was said."[177] So, yes, in addition to the content and form of the words, the Senate is obliged to consider the context, based on the whole record. (But not instead of it.)

---

175 *Id.* at 107 (quoting Gooding v. Wilson, 405 U.S. 518, 521–22 (1972)) (internal quotation marks omitted; emphasis added).

176 *Id.* at 109 (quoting the Indiana court's rationale) (emphasis added).

177 *Snyder v. Phelps*, 562 U.S. 443, 453 – 54 (2011) (internal quotation marks and citations omitted).

Here, of course, the "whole record" consists of the charges in the Article. An article of impeachment is literally a "charge" of particular wrongdoing. Thus, under the division of responsibility in the Constitution, the Senate must conduct a trial solely on the charge specified in articles of impeachment approved by a vote of the House and presented to the Senate. The Senate cannot expand the scope of a trial to consider mere assertions appearing in biased media reports that the House did not include in the articles of impeachment submitted to a vote of that Chamber, nor even in the unsupported statements in the House Managers' Trial Memorandum. Similarly, House Managers trying the case in the Senate must be confined to the specific conduct alleged in the Articles approved by the House. These restrictions follow both from the plain terms of the Constitution limiting the Senate to trying an "impeachment" framed by the House and from elementary principles of due process. "[T]he senator's role is solely one of acting on the accusations (Articles of Impeachment) voted by the House of Representatives. The Senate cannot lawfully find the president guilty of something not charged by the House, any more than a trial jury can find a defendant guilty of something not charged in the indictment." "No principle of procedural due process is more clearly established than that notice of the specific charge, and a chance to be heard in a trial of the issues raised by that charge, if desired, are among the constitutional rights of every accused."[178]

As the Supreme Court has explained, it has been the rule for over 130 years that "a court cannot permit a defendant to be tried on charges that are not made in the indictment against him."[179]

---

178 *Cole v. Arkansas*, 333 U.S. 196, 201 (1948).

179 *Stirone v. United States*, 361 U.S. 212, 217 (1960).

Doing so is "fatal error."[180] Under the same principles of due process, the Senate must similarly refuse to consider any uncharged allegations as a basis for conviction.

In its examination of context, the *Snyder* Court held that because the speech was protected, its setting, or context, could not render it unprotected.[181] In fact, Mr. Trump's admonition not to harm is analogous to the circumstance considered in *Bible Believers* as neutralizing the inciting tendency of words that were even more offensive in nature and delivered in an even more volatile context.

Even taking every one of Mr. Trump's prior statements about the election in the most negative light, they were, at most, only abstract discussions that never advocated for physical force. And even if they had broached the idea of violence, "the mere abstract teaching ... of the moral propriety or even moral necessity for a resort to force and violence, is not the same as preparing a group for violent action and steeling it to such action."[182] Indeed there had never been violence before and so there was thus no reason to expect that Mr. Trump's statements would lead to any injury to the officers or protesters. Moreover, even, assuming *arguendo*, if one could posit that the likely response to that statement would have been "imminent lawless action,"[183] Mr. Trump corrected any such misunderstanding by immediately saying "Stay Peaceful!"

The fact that some small percentage of unlawful rioters who, as the FBI already knew in advance, had been planning to come and wage war, did so later that same day, does not in any way mean that they were acting at Mr. Trump's direction or through any "incitement" from Mr. Trump.

---

180 *Id.*

181 *Snyder*, 562 U.S. at 454–55.

182 *Noto v. United States*, 367 U.S. 290, 298 (1961).

183 *Brandenburg*, 395 U.S. at 447.

In the context of ordinary civil litigation, such a "bald" allegation of agency "is by itself a mere legal conclusion and is therefore insufficient to withstand a motion to dismiss."[184] "A complaint relying on agency must plead facts which, if proved, could establish the existence of an agency relationship. It is insufficient to merely plead the legal conclusion of agency."[185] "Neither a single incident nor sporadic incidents are sufficient to establish foreseeability."[186]

For First Amendment purposes, the meaning of words must be judged objectively. Unprotected speech is the exception to the rule of free speech, so it cannot be punished on the ground that it might be unprotected. The speech must objectively fall within the narrow exception for unprotected speech, lest protected speech be penalized based on a subjective or idiosyncratic interpretation.[187] Courts "weigh the circumstances in order to protect, not to destroy, freedom of speech."[188] "[I]f the freedoms of expression are to have the breathing space that they need to survive,"[189] courts must "err on the side of protecting political speech."[190] Here, the question is not even close. Mr. Trump's words are core speech protected under the First Amendment.

---

184 *Prochaska & Associates, Inc. v. Merrill Lynch Pierce Fenner & Smith, Inc.*, 798 F.Supp. 1427, 1433 (D. Neb. 1992).

185 *Bird v. Delacruz*, 2005 WL 1625303, at *4 (S.D. Ohio July 6, 2005); *see also Nuevo Mundo Holdings v. PriceWaterhouseCoopers LLP*, 2004 WL 112948, at *6 (S.D.N.Y. 2004).

186 *Grisham v. Wal-Mart Stores, Inc.*, 929 F.Supp. 1054, 1058 (E.D. Ky. 1995), aff'd sub nom., 89 F.3d 833 (6th Cir. 1996).

187 *See Claiborne*, 458 U.S. at 915 n.50.

188 *Cox v. Louisiana*, 379 U.S. 536, 578 (1965) (Black, J, concurring); *Bible Believers*, 805 F.3d at 234 ("We interpret the First Amendment broadly so as to favor allowing more speech.").

189 *New York Times Co.* ,376 U.S. at 271-72.

190 *FEC v. Wisconsin Right to Life, Inc.*, 551 U.S. 449, 457 (2007).

4. Lastly, Mr. Trump's Figurative Use of the Words "Fight," "Fighting," Have Been Used By Many, None Are Impeachable

It is truly incredible that House Democratic leadership is feigning horror at the President's choices of words considering some of their own members recent public comments. For example, in 2018, Speaker Nancy Pelosi held her weekly press conference in the Capitol Visitor Center. In reference to a policy she disagreed with, the most powerful Democrat in the Country said: "I just don't even know why there aren't uprisings all over the country. Maybe there will be."[191] Was she advocating violence? Sending a silent dog whistle to radical protesters? Should she be held accountable for her extremist rhetoric and removed from office?

As political violence grew last summer, Representative Ayana Pressley went on national TV and said that "there needs to be unrest in the streets." Should we hold her liable to pay for all of the businesses that were destroyed when people heeded her call and removed from office ?[192]

In perhaps the most egregious call for physical confrontation, Rep Maxine Waters told a crowd at a rally that they should accost members of the government that they do not like.

> You think we're rallying now? You ain't seen nothing yet…Already you have members of your Cabinet that are being booed out of restaurants ... protesters taking up at their house saying 'no peace, no sleep…If you see anybody from that Cabinet in a restaurant, in a department store, at a gasoline station, you get out and you create a crowd and you push back on them and you tell them they're not welcome anymore, anywhere… We want history to record that we stood up, that we pushed back, that we fought…

---

191 Douglas Ernst, *Nancy Pelosi wonders why there 'aren't uprisings' across nation: 'Maybe there will be,'* The Washington Times (Jun. 14, 2018), https://www.washingtontimes.com/news/2018/jun/14/nancy-pelosi-wonders-why-there-arent-uprisings-acr/

192 Am Joy, *Post Office Cuts Are War Against American People Pressley Says*, MSNBC (Aug. 15, 2020), https://www.msnbc.com/am-joy/watch/post-office-cuts-are-war-against-american-people-pressley-says-90125893871

In another cable interview Waters was even more specific:

> I have no sympathy for these people that are in this administration … they won't be able to go to a restaurant, they won't be able to stop at a gas station, they're not going to be able to shop at a department store. The people are going to turn on them. They're going to protest. They're absolutely going to harass them…We've got to push back.

In that instance, even Speaker Pelosi called Representative Waters' remarks "unacceptable" but of course did nothing to remove her from office, just like she has done nothing to censure other Members who have tweeted calls for genocide[193] – because when it is her side of the aisle making their 'political speech' heard, Speaker Pelosi is nothing if not tolerant. Other Democratic leadership went so far as to defend Representative Waters by bending over backwards to read an inverted message of peacefulness into her violent statements – the *exact opposite* of what they did to former President Trump. Giving her far more than the benefit of the doubt, Representative Cedric Richmond claimed that "[i]n exercising her constitutional right to freedom of speech at a recent rally, Congresswoman Waters did not, as she has made clear, encourage violence . . . She instead, encouraged Americans to exercise their constitutional rights to freedom of speech and peaceful assembly…" For those who would say that those quotes must be understood in their greater context, *i.e.*, that they were clearly meant to be political speech- we say *exactly*. The truth is that both the Mr. Trump's speech and these comments are acceptable political free speech; it is the double standard at play here that is entirely unacceptable, and Mr. Trump ask that the Senate reject it in no uncertain terms.

---

[193] Aaron Bandler, *Rashida Tlaib Retweets 'From the River to the Sea'Tweet,* Jewish Journal (Nov. 30, 2020), https://jewishjournal.com/news/325415/rashida-tlaib-retweets-from-the-river-to-the-sea-tweet/

This is not the first time that Congress has impeached and tried to convict a President for making a speech, and the last time did not work either. The tenth Article of Impeachment against Andrew Johnson read as follows:

> That said Andrew Johnson, President of the United States, unmindful of the high duties of his office and the dignity and proprieties thereof, and of the harmony and courtesies which ought to exist and be maintained between the executive and legislative branches of the government of the United States, designing and intending to set aside the rightful authority and powers of Congress, did attempt to bring into disgrace, ridicule, hatred, contempt and reproach the Congress of the United States, and the several branches thereof, to impair and destroy the regard and respect of all the good people of the United States for the Congress and legislative power thereof (which all officers of the government ought inviolably to preserve and maintain,) and to excite the odium and resentment of all the good people of the United States against Congress and the laws by it duly and constitutionally enacted; and in pursuance of his said design and intent, openly and publicly, and before divers assemblages of the citizens of the United States convened in divers parts thereof to meet and receive said Andrew Johnson as the Chief Magistrate of the United States, did, ... make and deliver with a loud voice certain intemperate, inflammatory[,] and scandalous harangues, and did therein utter loud threats and bitter menaces as well against Congress as the laws of the United States duly enacted thereby, amid the cries[,] jeers[,] and laughter of the multitudes ... Which said utterances, declarations, threats[,] and harangues, highly censurable in any, are peculiarly indecent and unbecoming in the Chief Magistrate of the United States[.

While no vote was ever taken on the tenth Article, multiple Senators expressed their concern about trying to impeach for inflammatory rhetoric. James Patterson noted that "in view of the liberty of speech which our laws authorize, in view of the culpable license of speech which is practiced and allowed in other branches of the Government, I doubt if we can at present make low and scurrilous speeches a ground of impeachment."[194] Senator Sherman echoed this view;

---

[194] CONG. GLOBE, 40th Cong., 2d Sess. 509 (Supp. 1868); *see also* Shaw, *Impeachable Speech*, 70 Emory L.J. 1, 21.

while indicating his support for conviction on a number of the other articles, he voiced concerns about the tenth article, arguing that "we must guard against making crimes out of mere political differences or the abuse of the freedom of speech."[195]

D. The House Afforded President Trump No Due Process of Law

On January 12th, Speaker Pelosi announced the nine representatives who would serve as the impeachment managers. On January 13, 2021, mere days after the press conference purportedly launching the inquiry, House Democrats completed the fastest presidential impeachment inquiry in history and adopted the Article of Impeachment over strong opposition and with zero due process of law afforded to the President, against Constitutional requirements and centuries of practice. The lack of due process is no small matter; due process of law is not a formality it is a

---

195 *Impeachable Speech*, 70 Emory L.J. at 62:

> There have also been recent suggestions that the invocation of presidential speech in a trial setting raises First Amendment concerns. Judge Kozinski made this claim in an opinion regarding one of the challenges to President Trump's first "travel ban" executive order. *Washington v. Trump*, 858 F.3d 1168, 1173 (9th Cir. 2017) (Kozinski, J., dissenting). Dissenting from the denial of rehearing en banc, Judge Kozinski criticized the panel for citing "a trove of informal and unofficial statements from the President and his advisers." *Id.* This approach, Kozinski warned, threatened to "chill campaign speech, despite the fact that our most basic free speech principles have their 'fullest and most urgent application precisely to the conduct of campaigns for political office.'" *Id.* (citing *McCutcheon v. FEC*, 572 U.S. 185, 191-192 (2014)). Given the near-constant campaigning in which an incumbent president might engage, this argument could be extended to virtually every statement a president makes--including in the context of an impeachment inquiry.

See also Paul F. Campos, *A Constitution for the Age of Demagogues: Using the Twenty-Fifth Amendment to Remove an Unfit President*, 97 Denv. L. Rev. 85, 100 (2019), noting that "Impeachment, in practice, has become something intended solely to remove a corrupt president…"; and Bushnell, Eleanore. *Crimes, Follies, and Misfortunes: The Federal Impeachment Trials*. University of Illinois Press, 1992, p. 6, noting that "The impeachment procedure was designed to provide a means for removing a deficient officer, not to punish for derelictions of duty or substitute for a court trial. Therefore, it might seem obvious that no action need be taken when a suspect occupant removed himself from his position."

key Constitutional right, and when it is lacking a case is tainted and the case should be dismissed. In the civil context, the law is clear that a case should be dismissed if the government wrongfully interfered with a defendant's due process rights, and that "[a]t the core of procedural due process jurisprudence is the right to advance notice of significant deprivations of liberty or property and to a meaningful opportunity to be heard." *Abbott v. Latshaw*, 164 F.3d 141, 146 (3d Cir.1998).

As it relates to impeachment proceedings, the legal analog is clear:

> The gravity of the deprivation at stake in an impeachment—especially a presidential impeachment—buttresses the conclusion that some due process limitations must apply. It would be incompatible with the Framers' understanding of the "delicacy and magnitude of a trust which so deeply concerns the political reputation and existence of every man engaged in the administration of public affairs"[196] to think that they envisioned a system in which the House was free to devise any arbitrary or unfair mechanism it wished for impeaching individuals. The Supreme Court has described due process as "the protection of the individual against arbitrary action."[197] There is no reason to think that protection was not intended to extend to impeachments.[198]

And in terms of longstanding historical practice when it comes to those proceedings, the precedent is also unambiguous:

> Although constitutional requirements governing House impeachment proceedings may have been unsettled when the Constitution was adopted, by the 1870s consistent practice in the House (unbroken since then) gave meaning to the Constitution and settled the minimum procedures that must be afforded for a fair impeachment inquiry. The Framers, who debated impeachment with reference to the contemporaneous English impeachment of Warren

196 *The Federalist* No. 65, *supra* note at 397 (Alexander Hamilton).

197 *Ohio Bell Tel. Co. v. Pub. Serv. Comm'n*, 301 U.S. 292, 302 (1937).

198 Trial Memorandum of President Donald J. Trump (2020); *Hastings v. United States*, 802 F. Supp. 490, 504 (D.D.C. 1992), *vacated and remanded on other grounds by Hastings v. United States*, 988 F.2d 1280 (D.C. Cir. 1993) (per curiam).

> Hastings,[199] knew that "the House of Commons did hear the accused, and did permit him to produce testimony, before they voted an impeachment against him."[200] And practice in the United States rapidly established that the accused in an impeachment must be allowed fair process. Although a few early impeachment investigations were *ex parte*,[201] the House provided the accused with notice and an opportunity to be heard in the majority of cases starting as early as 1818.[202]

Democratic Members of the House have argued that then-President Trump's alleged offense was so grave and his power so immense that there was no time to wait for the actual facts to come to light. In a crocodile-tear-stained letter, Representative Ilhan Omar, herself no stranger to extremist rhetoric,[203] exhorted her colleagues by saying, "The urgency of this moment is real and we have to be courageous and unified in defense of our Republic…Every single hour that Donald Trump remains in office, our country, our democracy, and our national security remain in danger. Congress must take immediate action to keep the people of this country safe and set a precedent

---

199 2 *Records of the Federal Convention of 1787*, at 550 (M. Farrand ed. 1966); *see, e.g.*, Richard M. Pious, *Impeaching the President: The Intersection of Constitutional and Popular Law*, 43 St. Louis L.J. 859, 872 (1999); *see also, e.g.*, *Proceedings of the Senate Sitting for the Trial of William W. Belknap, Late Secretary of War, on the Articles of Impeachment Exhibited by the House of Representatives*, 44th Cong. 98 (1876) (statement of Sen. Timothy Howe); Scott S. Barker, *An Overview of Presidential Impeachment*, 47 Colo. Lawyer 30, 32 (Sept. 2018).

200 6 Reg. Deb. 737 (1830) (statement of Rep. James Buchanan).

201 *See* III Hinds' Precedents § 2319, at 681 (Judge Pickering); *id.* § 2343, at 716 (Justice Chase).

202 *See* 32 Annals of Cong. 1715, 1715–16 (1818); *see, e.g.*, III Hinds' Precedents § 2491, at 988 (Judge Thurston, 1825); *id.* § 1736, at 97–98 (Vice President Calhoun, 1826); *id.* §§ 2365–2366 (Judge Peck, 1830–1831); *id.* § 2491, at 989 (Judge Thurston, 1837); *id.* § 2495, at 994 & n.4 (Judge Watrous, 1852); Cong. Globe, 35th Cong., 1st Sess. 2167 (1858) (statement of Rep. Horace Clark) (Judge Watrous, 1858); III Hinds' Precedents § 2496, at 999 (Judge Watrous, 1858); *id.* § 2504, at 1008 (Judge Delahay, 1873).

203 Sarah Elbeshbishi, Nicholas Wu, *GOP targets Ihan Omar after Dems try to Oust Majorie Taylor Green,* USA Today (Feb. 4, 2021), https://www.usatoday.com/story/news/politics/2021/02/03/gop-targets-ilhan-omar-after-dems-try-oust-marjorie-taylor-green/4369715001/ and Rep Andy Biggs, Twitter (Feb. 3, 2021, 9:02 AM), https://twitter.com/RepAndyBiggsAZ/status/1356966391493111808.

that such behavior cannot be tolerated." Of course, President Trump's term came to an end without the apocalyptic predictions of the all-seeing Rep. Omar coming to pass.

As Speaker Pelosi told the country, she had to act *now* "so urgent was the matter." So urgent, of course, that instead of immediately sending it over to the Senate so that the President could have a trial and, if convicted, be removed, the Speaker once again decided to act in a purely political manner, pretending that she was rushing the impeachment to protect the country from an imminent danger, and then waiting until the President was no longer in the White House to prefer the charge. The House actually took longer t o transmit the Article of Impeachment to the Senate than it did to investigate and debate it in the first place.

Of course, this is not the first time that Speaker Pelosi has ignored the Constitutional protections in an impeachment proceeding. When they led the impeachment of then-President Trump the first time, the Democratic leadership also denied him due process (although not as brazenly and outrageously as this time) and the Speaker also refused to send the Articles of Impeachment to the Senate right away. That time, her machinations were focused on trying to influence the rules that the Senate would put in place for the trial, and she only sent the articles to the Senate when it became clear that she would not get her way. [204] But, just like this time, in withholding the articles the Speaker undercut one of her party's "primary arguments for impeachment in the first place: the need for urgency in removing Trump."[205] As Democratic

---

204 John Hulsman, *In the impeachment saga trump derangement syndrome is destroying the Democrats*, City A.M. (Jan. 20, 2020), https://www.cityam.com/in-the-impeachment-saga-trump-derangement-syndrome-is-destroying-the-democrats/ ("Republican Senate majority leader Mitch McConnell, as shrewd a tactician as Pelosi herself, had the speaker's number, and he has been grimly clear in response to the issue of Pelosi trying to leverage him: "We will not cede our (Senate) authority to try this impeachment. The House Democrats' turn is over.")

205 *Id.*

senator and staunch Pelosi ally Dianne Feinstein put it: "'The longer it goes on, the less urgent it becomes. So if it's serious and urgent, send them over. If it isn't, don't send it over.'"[206]

This time the Speaker apparently held the Articles over so that she could effectively, maneuver an ally in the Senate into the judge's chair. Once the 45th President's term expired, and the House chose to allow jurisdiction to lapse on the Article of Impeachment, the constitutional mandate for the Chief Justice to preside at all impeachments involving the President disappears. Now, instead of the Chief Justice, the trial will be overseen by a biased and partisan Senator who will purportedly *also act as a juror* while ruling on issues that arise during trial.

The Senate, in reviewing the House actions, should immediately dismiss this case because the process was completely unfair and one-sided. The civil analog is clear: "Every federal appellate court has a special obligation to 'satisfy itself not only of its own jurisdiction, but also that of the lower courts in a cause under review,' even though the parties are prepared to concede it."[207]

Throughout this entire process Speaker Pelosi was never acting to apply her understanding of the laws of impeachment in any principled manner. The Speaker did *not* think it was necessary to call for an impeachment so long as she got her way, and twice told the Vice President, and the country, just that. She did *not* really believe that the process was "urgent" and it was *never* actually about whether President Donald Trump would stay in office, because once she brought the impeachment Article to a vote she decided to hold it until after he had finished the remainder of his term. If the Speaker really believed that the President was that much of a danger, then she was being criminally negligent by holding it back. Obviously, as demonstrated by her actions, there

---

206 *Id.*

207 *Steel Co. v. Citizens for a Better Env't*, 523 U.S. 83, 95, 118 S. Ct. 1003, 1013 (1998) (interior quotation omitted).

was only ever one urgency, to score political points quickly before the harried Members of even her own party could calm down and look at the facts. And there was only ever one motivation; to try and spin this incredibly sad moment in American history, and use it to embarrass the President. Unfortunately for House Democrats, the impeachment of a former United States President, a private citizen, is unconstitutional.

E. The Article Is Structurally Deficient and Can Only Result in Acquittal.

The hastily drafted Article is not only wrong on the facts and the law, it also suffers from a Constitutionally fatal structural defect that the Senate cannot remedy. This defect alone makes it worthy of dismissal:

> Put simply, the articles are impermissibly duplicitous—that is, each article charges multiple different acts as possible grounds for sustaining a conviction.[208] The problem with an article offering such a menu of options is that the Constitution requires two-thirds of Senators present to agree ***on the specific basis for conviction***. A vote on a duplicitous article, however, could never provide certainty that a two-thirds majority had actually agreed upon a ground for conviction. Instead, such a vote could be the product of an amalgamation of votes resting on several different theories, no single one of which would have garnered two-thirds support if it had been presented separately. Accordingly, duplicitous articles like those exhibited here are facially unconstitutional.[209]

As noted in our previously filed Answer to the Charges, by charging multiple alleged wrongs in one article, the House of Representatives has made it impossible to guarantee compliance with the Constitutional mandate in Article 1, Sec. 3, Cl. 6 that permits a conviction only by at least two-thirds of the members. The House charge fails by interweaving differing allegations rather than

---

208 "'Duplicity' is the joining of two or more distinct and separate offenses in a single count"; "'[m]ultiplicity' is charging a single offense in several counts." 1A Charles Alan Wright et al., *Federal Practice and Procedure* § 142 (4th ed. 2019); *see, e.g.*, *United States v. Root*, 585 F.3d 145, 150 (3d Cir. 2009); *United States v. Chrane*, 529 F.2d 1236, 1237 n.3 (5th Cir. 1976).

209 House Trial Memo 2020.

breaking them out into counts of alleged individual instances of misconduct. Rule XXIII of the *Rules of Procedure and Practice in the Senate When Sitting on Impeachment Trials* provides, in pertinent part, that an article of impeachment shall not be divisible thereon. Because the Article at issue here alleges multiple wrongs in the single article, it would be impossible to know if two-thirds of the members agreed on the entire article, or just on parts, as the basis for vote to convict. The House failed to adhere to strict Senate rules and, instead, chose to make the Article as broad as possible intentionally in the hope that some Senators might agree with parts, and other Senators agree with other parts, but that when these groups of senators were added together, the House might achieve the appearance of two thirds in agreement, when those two thirds of members, in reality, did not concur on the *same* allegations interwoven into an over-broad article designed for just such a purpose.

F. The Article Fails to State an Impeachable Offense as a Matter of Law.

The Articles of Impeachment also fail because, as former D.C. Assistant Attorney General Jeffrey Scott Shapiro explains, "**The president didn't commit incitement or any other crime.**" As it relates to the allegation in the Article:

> In the District of Columbia, it's a crime to "intentionally or recklessly act in such a manner to cause another person to be in reasonable fear" and to "incite or provoke violence where there is a likelihood that such violence will ensue... The president didn't mention violence on Wednesday, much less provoke or incite it. He said, "I know that everyone here will soon be marching over to the Capitol building to peacefully and patriotically make your voices heard." District law defines a riot as "a public disturbance . . . which by tumultuous and violent conduct or the threat thereof creates grave danger of damage or injury to property or persons." When Mr. Trump spoke, there was no "public disturbance," only a rally. The "disturbance" came later at the Capitol by a small minority who entered the perimeter and broke the law. The president's critics want him charged for inflaming the emotions of angry Americans. That alone does not satisfy the elements of any criminal offense, and

> therefore his speech is protected by the Constitution that members of Congress are sworn to support and defend.[210]

It matters greatly that the President did not commit a crime, because the Constitutional requirement for action that is grounds for impeachment is a high crime or misdemeanor.

> By limiting impeachment to cases of "Treason, Bribery, or other high Crimes and Misdemeanors,"[211] the Framers restricted impeachment to specific offenses against "already known and established law."[212] That was a deliberate choice designed to constrain the impeachment power. In keeping with that restriction, every prior presidential impeachment in our history has been based on alleged violations of existing law—indeed, criminal law...[213] **The terminology of "high Crimes and Misdemeanors" makes clear that an impeachable offense must be a violation of established law.** The Impeachment Clause did not confer upon Congress a roving license to make up new standards of conduct for government officials and to permit removal from office merely on a conclusion that conduct was "bad" if there was not an existing law that it violated. [214]

House Democrats' theory on insurrection collapses at the threshold because it fails to describe any violation of law whatsoever. Aside from the decided lack of causation that the evidence *demonstrably* proves,[215] Mr. Trump's speech was well-within the long-understood protection of

---

210 Jeffrey Scott Shapiro, *No, Trump Isn't Guilty of Incitement*, Wall Street Journal (Jan. 10, 2021), https://www.wsj.com/articles/no-trump-isnt-guilty-of-incitement-11610303966

211 U.S. Const., art. II, § 4.

212 4 William Blackstone, *Commentaries on the Laws of England* *256.

213 *See Impeachment Inquiry into President Donald J. Trump: Constitutional Grounds for Presidential Impeachment Before the H.R. Comm. on the Judiciary*, 116th Cong. (2019) (written statement of Professor Jonathan Turley, Geo. Wash. Univ. Law Sch., at 15, https://perma.cc/QU4H-FZC4); H.R. Res. 611, 106th Cong. (1998); H.R. Comm. on the Judiciary, *Impeachment of William Jefferson Clinton, President of the United States*, H.R. Rep. No. 105-830, 105th Cong. 143 (1998) (additional views of Rep. Bill McCollum); H.R. Comm. on the Judiciary, *Impeachment of Richard M. Nixon, President of the United States*, H.R. Rep. No. 93-1305, 93d Cong. 1–3 (1974).

214 House Trial Memo 2020.

215 See timeline above and see FBI reports.

the First Amendment. A person does not lose his fundamental right to speak his mind just because he is the President.

IV. CONCLUSION

The Article of Impeachment presented by the House is unconstitutional for a variety of reasons, any of which alone would be grounds for immediate dismissal. Taken together, they demonstrate conclusively that indulging House Democrats hunger for this political theater is a danger to our Republic democracy and the rights that we hold dear. Reasons for dismissal include:

1. The Senate of the United States lacks jurisdiction over the 45th President because he holds no public office from which he can be removed, and the Constitution limits the authority of the Senate in cases of impeachment to removal from office as the prerequisite active remedy allowed the Senate under our Constitution.

2. The Senate of the United States lacks jurisdiction over the 45th President because he holds no public office from which he can be removed rendering the Article of Impeachment moot and a non-justiciable question.

3. Should the Senate act on the Article of Impeachment initiated in the House of Representatives, it will have passed a Bill of Attainder in violation of Article 1, Sec. 9. Cl. 3 of the United States Constitution.

4. The allegations in the Article of Impeachment are self-evidently wrong, as demonstrated by the evidence including the transcript of the President's actual speech, and the allegations fail to meet the constitutional standard for any crime, let alone an impeachable offense.

5. The House of Representatives deprived the 45th President of due process of law in rushing to issue the Article of Impeachment and by ignoring its own procedures and precedents going back to the mid-19th century. The lack of due process included, but was not limited to, its failure to conduct any meaningful committee review or other investigation, engage in any full and fair consideration of evidence in support of the Article, as well as the failure to conduct any full and fair discussion by allowing the 45th President's positions to be heard in the House Chamber. No exigent circumstances under the law were present excusing the House of Representatives' rush to judgment, as evidenced by the fact that they then held the Article for another 12 days.

6. The Article of Impeachment violates the 45th President's right to free speech and thought guaranteed under the First Amendment to the United States Constitution.

7. The Article is constitutionally flawed in that it charges multiple instances of allegedly impeachable conduct in a single article.

The Senate should dismiss these charges and acquit the President because this is clearly *not* what the Framers wanted or what the Constitution allows.

Respectfully submitted,

Bruce L. Castor, Jr.
David Schoen
Michael T. van der Veen
Counsel to the 45th President
of the United States

February 8, 2021

Made in United States
North Haven, CT
05 November 2026

21765615R00043